Investing for Business Value

How to Maximize the Strategic Benefits of Health Care Information Technology

Joseph M. DeLuca, FACHE, and Rebecca Enmark Cagan

AHA books are published by American Hospital Publishing, Inc., an American Hospital Association company

This publication is designed to provide accurate and authoritative information in regard to the subject matter covered. It is sold with the understanding that neither the authors nor the publisher is engaged in rendering legal, accounting, or other professional service. If legal advice or other expert assistance is required, the services of a competent professional should be sought.

The views expressed in this publication are strictly those of the authors and do not necessarily represent official positions of the American Hospital Association.

Library of Congress Cataloging-in-Publication Data

DeLuca, Joseph, 1956–
    Investing for business value : how to maximize the strategic
benefits of health care information technology / Joseph M. DeLuca
and Rebecca Enmark Cagan.
       p.   cm.
    Includes bibliographical references.
    ISBN 1-55648-170-5
    1. Health services administration—Data processing.
2. Information technology. 3. Information storage and retrieval
systems—Health services administration. 4. Health facilities—
Business administration. 5. Health services administration—Data
processing—Cost effectiveness. 6. Information storage and
retrieval systems—Health services administration—Cost
effectiveness. I. Cagan, Rebecca Enmark. II. Title.
RA971.6.E453   1996
362.1'068'4—dc20   96-42116
                                               CIP

Catalog no. 093107

AHA is a service mark of the American Hospital Association used under license by American Hospital Publishing, Inc.

Text set in English Times
2M—11/96—0451

Richard Hill, Senior Editor
Nancy Charpentier, Editor
Peggy DuMais, Assistant Production Manager
Marcia Bottoms, Director, Books Division

To Marsha J. Broquedis and Eric Cagan,
our beloved spouses, for their endless tolerance,
support, and encouragement over the course of this effort.

Contents

List of Figures and Tables

Tables

About the Authors

Joseph M. DeLuca, FACHE, is founder and CEO of Health Care Investment Visions, LLC in Alameda, California, which provides advisory, financial, and research services to companies involved in developing, funding, and implementing health care information technologies (ITs). He has worked closely with national health care leaders in the design and implementation of integrated delivery systems, focusing on the strategic use of information systems technology to support business and medical service requirements. Prior to founding Health Care Investment Visions, LLC, Mr. DeLuca founded and managed JDA, a health care technology consulting firm in San Francisco. During his decade-long tenure as JDA president, he acted in an advisory role to provider organizations of all sizes and orientations, including acute care, pediatric, research, and university hospitals; integrated delivery systems; medical groups; and managed care organizations.

A frequent speaker at regional and national conferences, Mr. DeLuca is widely published on IT topics in industry journals and monographs. His first book (with Owen Doyle), *Health Care Information Systems: An Executive's Guide for Successful Management,* was published by American Hospital Publishing in 1991. A reformation of that work, *The CEO's Guide to Health Care Information Systems* (with Rebecca Enmark Cagan), was issued in mid-1996.

A fellow in the American College of Healthcare Executives, Mr. DeLuca holds a master's degree in health services administration from the University of Wisconsin at Madison and a bachelor of arts degree in biology, magna cum laude, from Lawrence University in Appleton, Wisconsin. Over the course of his career, he has worked in the direct management of health care facilities, business/medical service and IT consulting, and information systems product development and market entry, as well as emerging technology feasibility planning.

Rebecca Enmark Cagan is research manager for Health Care Investment Visions in Alameda, California. She is responsible for corporate research activities as well as education and publishing programs. Ms. Cagan specializes in IT research and market analysis, surveying products and vendors serving the health care industry. Formerly, as research associate at JDA, she developed and maintained the industry research base, a comprehensive collection of product and vendor information covering nearly 1,000 commercial health care IT vendors.

Previous works by Ms. Cagan include *Quality Measurement Systems: Strategies, Product Profiles and Healthcare Information Systems Capabilities* (JDA, 1994) and *The CEO's Guide to Health Care Information Systems* (American Hospital Publishing, 1996).

Ms. Cagan holds a master's degree in library and information studies and a bachelor's degree in English literature from the University of California at Berkeley. Over the course of her career, she has directed research and analysis activities on subjects including information technology, labor markets, and postsecondary education.

Health Care Investment Visions, LLC provides advisory services for early stage, mature, or "in concept" health care information technology companies or capital sources. Services offered by Health Care Investment Visions, LLC bring together practical health care market knowledge, innovative entrepreneurial experience, execution capabilities, and research skills to enable the *intelligent application* of capital, technology, product, and human resources.

JDA is a health care information technology consulting firm focused on the use and advancement of information technology by provider organizations. Since 1995, JDA has been a wholly owned subsidiary of Science Applications International Corporation (SAIC), an international systems integration firm. SAIC provides systems integration, research, and applied scientific services to the government and private sectors in the areas of health care, national security, energy, environment, transportation, and systems integration.

Preface

The explosion of information technology into daily life has been continual and overwhelming. In every area, technological potential is stretching the limits of what individuals, groups, and corporations can accomplish. As our use of these new capabilities becomes more sophisticated, and our understanding more mature, the goal of technology for its own sake falls by the wayside. Today's technology user seeks—and often demands—measurable value from IT investments. Finding that value is becoming a subject of increasing concern and debate.

Some types of health care IT have established return on investment (ROI)—clear, intuitive rationale for business investments. Other types remain murky. It is our hope that this work will contribute to the investment/return dialogue, expanding the body of thought, knowledge, and perspective, assisting you as executive management to understand and participate in this debate.

Preparing for Change

The health care industry in the United States is at an unparalleled moment of change. Pressure to contain the growth of expenditures and decrease the per capita cost of health care, while simultaneously increasing access and expanding service coverage, will accelerate in the next decade. The current lack of national momentum for comprehensive Medicare, Medicaid, and private-sector health care reform will not diminish reform initiatives. Most likely, local and state efforts will fill this vacuum—driven by business coalitions, employers, payers, and recipients of care demanding high-quality health care at an affordable cost.

As market demands and health care delivery grow increasingly complex and sophisticated, provider constituents are successfully pressuring for more control of health care delivery and quality. Purchasers and employers are demanding cost containment; consumers, more knowledgeable than in the past, are concerning themselves with quality, access, and service issues;

and legislators at local, state, and federal levels are responding to these concerns with threats of fundamental reform.

Outpatient, home health, and physician practice services continue to displace the traditional reliance on inpatient care. The increasing impact of managed care and capitation on care service and reimbursement is being felt across the country. Providers, struggling with increased risk assumption, are joining with payers and employers in the effort to develop quantitative cost and quality measurement tools. Nationally, there is an explosion in the formation of regional integrated health delivery systems. Organizations across the continuum of care are struggling to adapt to market reform and to create a viable provider infrastructure for the next generation of health care delivery. These changes, together with a number of emerging and ongoing trends, all affect the data and information needs of provider organizations.

Few health care professionals, including top executives, can predict with confidence the results of these changes. In the next decade, however, those organizations that do not prepare well for change, introducing and sustaining a strong balance between cost and quality, will cease to exist.

Understanding the Role of Information Technology

Ironically, health care information technology (IT), one of the most effective strategic and tactical tools available, remains largely underestimated, misunderstood, and underutilized. Non–health care industries use IT to develop and sustain price, product, market, or production competitive advantages through activities such as strategy formulation, market analysis, production control, quality control/management, and transaction cost reduction.

In health care, although most modern executives have learned to comprehend complex economic and market analysis about their delivery systems, many are not as conversant about IT and its medical and business applications. Some executives view the information systems department as a data-processing unit; others acknowledge the importance of "knowing technology" but lack the necessary skill base.

Such executives and organizations are at an increasing disadvantage in the market. They may be unable to effectively discern the difference between an IT investment's *business value* (what benefits the investment is capable of producing) and its *specific utility* (how well system capabilities are being used by an organization). Although these concepts are clearly linked, they represent distinct perspectives.

To achieve maximum utility from an IT investment, the modern health care executive must first conceptualize and plan for its business value. Far too often, we encounter a situation where an information system (IS) application—registration, laboratory, case management, managed care contracting—does not provide the specific utility (features, functions, capabilities, and new processes/procedures) to support the desired business value. A "gap" or misalignment exists. As a result, business goals and return on investment (ROI) expectations are not met. One goal of this book is to help executives maximize IT business value by illustrating documented, quantifiable benefits that are possible through IT investments.

Developing the Fundamental Skills

Over the next two years, health care information systems managers and chief information officers generally expect IT budgets to increase significantly. (See figure P-1.) Across the industry, health care IT investments are increasing in frequency and dollar value. Although certain IT unit costs (for example, hardware purchases) are declining, overall costs associated with IT are increasing. For some organizations, particularly health systems with complex geographic, payer, and provider structures, it is not unusual to see IT capital budgets exceed 50 percent of the organization's total capital budget.

Figure P-1. Planned IS Investment Budgets, Next Two Years

Survey Question: Which of the following best characterizes your planned IS budget for the next two years?

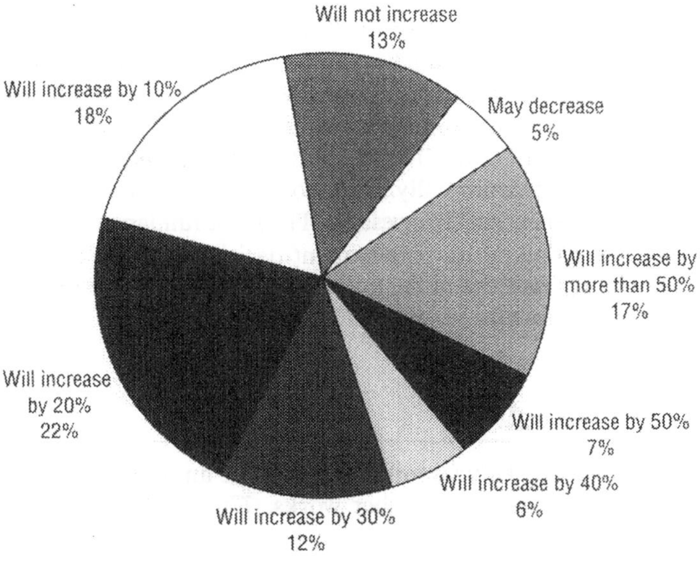

Source: Reprinted, with permission, from the 1996 HIMSS/Hewlett Packard Leadership Survey.

Successful providers will develop fundamental skills, or core competencies, in information management and movement (the preparation, collection, transport, retrieval, storage, access, presentation, and transformation of information in all its forms—voice, graphics, text, video, and image).* These specific skill sets—and their successful use in routine management activities—will, over time, create value for customers and constituencies, enhancing and supporting a competitive position. Contemporary business wisdom also indicates that well-developed core competencies eventually will evolve into areas of distinction—unique as well as extraordinary value—positioning an organization to offer aggressive, proactive value to customers. Such an ability creates a formidable, sustainable competitive advantage.

We have experienced core and distinct competencies in information management and movement in our client environments. Establishing these skills and knowledge sets to complement and enhance existing capabilities in clinical practices, management processes, and financial management requires a clear understanding of IT expectations and a developmental management philosophy supported by a clear plan. Core IS competencies can reach a critical mass in organizations, expanding exponentially the business value and specific utility of IT investments. As market demands grow in complexity and sophistication, superior health care providers will develop and exploit these competencies aggressively through all layers of the organization. *Investing for Business Value: How to Maximize the Strategic Benefits of Information Technology* provides leaders with some of the information needed to develop and maintain these competencies.

This book also concentrates on one specific aspect of the information management and IS delivery opportunity: maximization of economic and strategic IT benefits. Unfortunately, quantifying the benefits of an IT investment, in hard ROI terms, can be an elusive and frustrating task. Returns may manifest in different, even incomparable ways, making it difficult to evaluate an investment's overall worth and success. Yet market and budget pressures combine to continually make cost-benefit analysis an important priority and requirement of IT investing. The most fundamental and important question asked about any investment decision is quite appropriately: What good will this investment be to the organization? This book examines a composite set of factors to support an answer.

Using This Book

Investing for Business Value is not intended to be an introduction to health care information systems. Our other works, *The CEO's Guide to Health*

---

*Bernard Boar, *The Art of Strategic Planning for Information Technology* (New York City: John Wiley and Sons, 1993), p. 3.

Care Information Systems (AHPI, 1996) and *Health Care Information Systems: An Executive's Guide for Successful Management* (AHPI, 1991), provide enabling knowledge regarding health care IS strategic planning, systems implementation, and operations, as well as an overview of common health care information system applications; this work builds on the concepts introduced in those books (although this book can and does stand alone).* The logic of this work is fairly straightforward. The introductory chapters present distinct concepts of strategic IT benefits planning and the later chapters apply those theories to real-world technologies and provider organizations.

Chapter 1, "The Information Technology Benefit Framework," explores the technical and business forces that determine most health care providers' ROI expectations. It discusses specific investment attributes and behaviors, and how they contribute to an organization's ultimate ROI. It also discusses and defines the concepts of incremental and breakthrough benefits, and provides a conceptual model for evaluating ROI. The two most common IT development approaches, packaged software and custom development, are defined and compared from a potential ROI and risk/reward viewpoint. This chapter is designed to provide an overall strategic framework for benefits-based IT investment planning.

Chapter 2, "Realistic Return on Investment: Achievable Benefits of Information Technology," discusses the factors involved in setting realistic ROI goals for IT investments. After a brief discussion of macro technology benefits, the chapter focuses on the current and demonstrated benefits of information technology. Through synthesized benefits experiences, drawn from provider organizations across the country, this chapter provides a rich history of what has actually been accomplished with IT.

The types of technologies discussed in chapter 2 include: networking and telecommunications; electronic data interchange; general financial systems; patient financial and administrative systems; decision support systems; managed care systems; clinical systems; and ancillary department systems.

Chapter 3, "Emerging Technologies and Their Impact," guides provider organizations in the use and evaluation of emerging, unproven technologies. Such technologies, which are not currently "cost justified" in the health care market, necessitate special consideration from provider organizations. This chapter also addresses the question of when a technology is fully "emerged." Some of the technologies covered in this chapter include: electronic medical records; clinical workstations and bedside devices; patient imaging and optical systems; patient interactive systems; voice technology; and the Internet. The primary goals of this chapter are to communicate an understanding of the tactical issues related to unproven technology and

---

*For the advanced practitioner of technology long-range planning, we recommend Boar's *The Art of Strategic Planning for Information Technology.*

to articulate a usable framework for developing an emerging technology oversight program.

Chapter 4, "The Long-Range Plan: A Model for Maximum Returns," draws on the concepts and ideas presented in chapters 1 through 3 to develop a model long-range plan for an electronic medical record implementation project. The plan is based on an actual engagement conducted at Sharp HealthCare, in San Diego. The model plan is intended as a learning tool for readers and emphasizes:

- Performing an environmental review (identifying situational and organizational factors that may affect the project's success)
- Selecting the development and IT environment best suited to the project and the organization
- Quantifying the probable benefits of the project
- Identifying the risks involved with the technology and devising strategies to minimize them

Chapter 5, "Leadership for Achieving Breakthrough Benefits," reviews the strategic and tactical considerations in accomplishing breakthrough gains for the health care organization. This final chapter ties together the concepts of the book, focusing on the ongoing nature and characteristics of breakthrough strategies and benefits. Discussion topics emphasize:

- Reviewing the basic concepts and characteristics behind breakthrough investing
- Facilitating the achievement of breakthrough benefits
- Considering the elements involved in planning, reviewing, or initiating a potential breakthrough investment

This book also contains two appendixes. Appendix A, "IT Features, Functionalities, and Projected Benefits," expands on a concept discussed in chapter 2, illustrating in greater detail the connection between business problems and IT features/functionalities. Appendix B, "Sample Emerging Technology Oversight Group Charter," further delineates that concept as defined in chapter 3. The book concludes with a glossary of terms that appear in the book, as well as terms in general use in the health care and IT industries.

The material contained in this book will not make your strategic IT decisions or establish your IT ROI expectations for you; however, it will open your mind to the spectrum of benefits and the ROI continuum your organization can enjoy from the well-planned, well-implemented use of information technology.

Acknowledgments

No single professional can write a work of this depth alone. Over the past four years, a number of JDA consultants have directly contributed their health care and IT knowledge, experience, and guidance in the development of this project. In particular, we would like to thank Lee Penn, MBA, MPH, for developing early versions of chapter 3; and Edward Kopetsky, senior VP/CIO at Centura Health Support Center (formerly CEO and VP, information services, at Sharp HealthCare), Sandra McCullough, RN, Sharp HealthCare EMR/CDR committee chair, and Tom Mack, RPh, JDA project manager, for their efforts at Sharp HealthCare that formed the basis for chapter 4. We thank the management and staff at American Hospital Publishing, particularly Richard Hill and Nancy Charpentier, for their ongoing support and encouragement, as well as their invaluable comments on early publication drafts.

The Information Technology Benefit Framework

As a tool, information technology (IT) can be highly effective in meeting the new and emerging needs of health care delivery and financing—when the investment decision is well planned and wisely implemented. However, how organizations reach investment decisions, and the benefits they actually realize, can vary tremendously. This chapter outlines the technical and business forces that determine most health care providers' expectations for return on investment (ROI). These forces, together with specific investment attributes, behaviors, and decisions, produce an investment's ultimate return. Channeling these factors into a defined, analytical plan for maximizing ROI is called *benefits-based IT investment planning.*

The strategic management process for conducting benefits-based IT investment planning is relatively straightforward. (See figure 1-1.) As environmental pressures and technological trends trigger an organization's decision to explore a particular technology, the initial planning point is always any existing business, medical, and operations plans. These plans—and specific, defined IT requirements—are the basis for beginning to develop IT strategies that harmonize with overall organizational strategies and goals.

A number of steps, drivers, and influences contribute to the compilation of the formal benefits-based, long-range IT plan. All too often, organizations reacting blindly to internal or external imperatives sacrifice one or more of the middle steps of this process:[1]

- *Determine ROI expectations:* These expectations are influenced by factors both internal and external to the health care organization. This is an important step to execute because ROI expectations are a critical input into IT strategy formulation. Without a clear understanding of what the goals and expectations of an investment are to be, it is difficult—if not impossible—to achieve any positive returns cost-effectively.
- *Formulate principles and guidelines for IT investment:* Often these principles and guidelines exist at some level within an organization, but are "understood" rather than articulated. Formally documenting these investment standards is a valuable mechanism for focusing and sustaining

Figure 1-1. Forming Principles and Guidelines for IT Investment

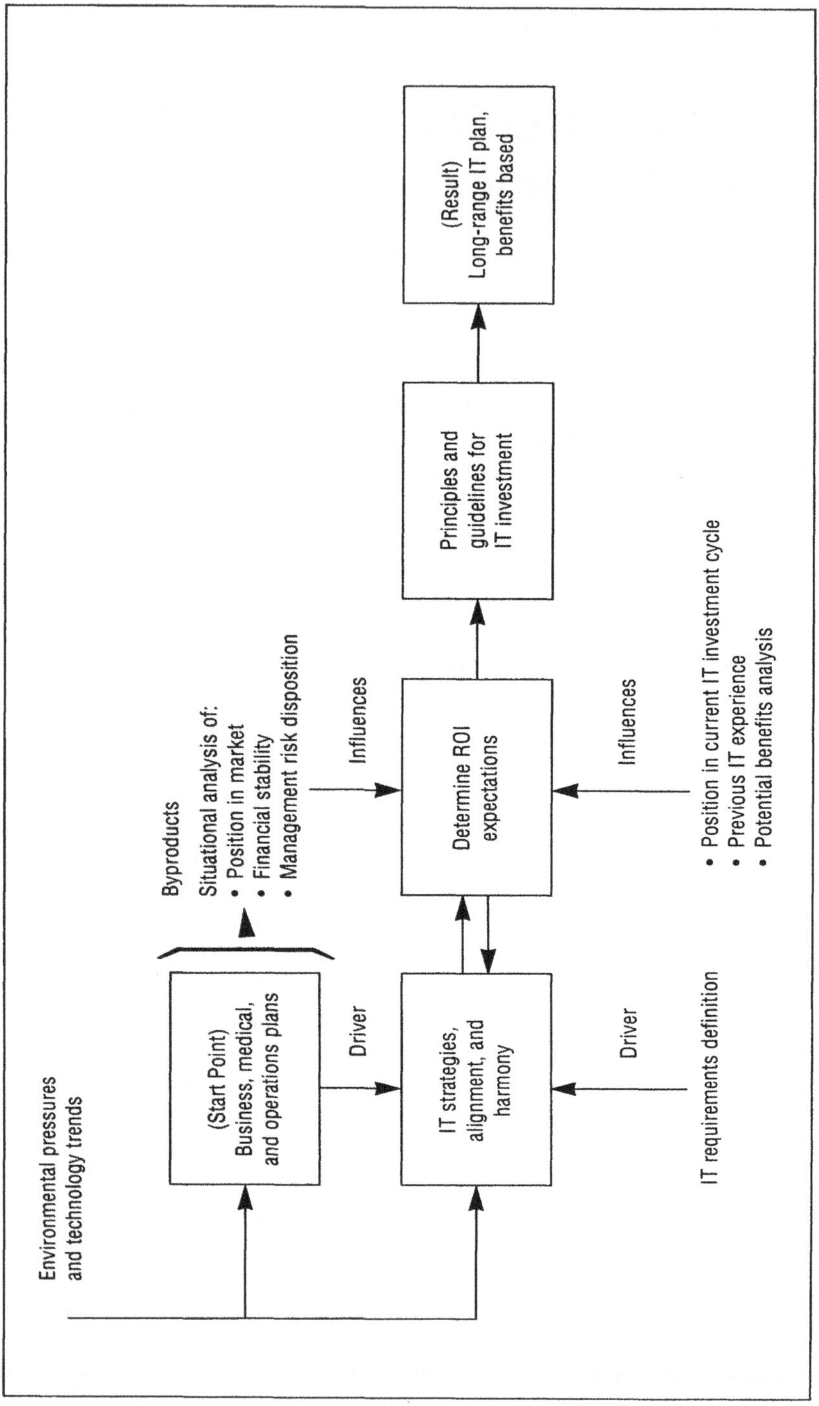

organizational momentum toward benefits realization. In addition, this step provides a knowledge-transfer mechanism that can be used to train and educate both current and future staff on the standards accepted by the organization.

Determining ROI Expectations

Analyzing, anticipating, and planning for IT benefits are the most important steps toward securing a positive return from any investment. As a rule, the overall approach an organization takes to investing in information technology will determine the extent and intensity of expected returns. A mathematical calculation to measure the benefit returns of an IT investment might look like this:

Return on Investment =

$$\sum_{\substack{\text{Years} \\ = 1}}^{N} \left(\frac{\text{Expected Quantifiable Economic Returns per Year}}{\substack{\text{Direct System Costs per Year} + \\ \text{Maintenance/Service per Year} + \\ \text{Cost of Funds per Year}}} + \substack{\text{Expected Strategic} \\ \text{Returns per Year}} \right),$$

where the anticipated costs and benefits from each year of the expected life of the investment are considered. *Expected quantifiable returns* are those cash or efficiency benefits that can be correlated directly to the technology investment. For example, an organization purchasing an automated contract management system may project the recovery of currently uncollected contract fees — fees not collected because the organization is unable to accurately monitor contract fee levels and payer compliance. As a result of the investment, the organization can logically expect to receive cash and earnings.

Expected strategic returns are those benefits that provide important positioning or infrastructure advantages, but are difficult or impossible to tie directly to a quantifiable gain. For example, an HMO investing in an automated enrollee outpatient scheduling system may project an increase in covered lives through their improved ability to meet service needs.

Although more difficult to measure, in some cases the strategic returns from an investment may manifest over a period of time longer than the actual useful life of the investment itself. An organization using IT to develop critical paths or case management capabilities for at-risk populations will find themselves at a strategic advantage even after the investment has lived out its useful lifespan — through reduced costs and better risk management capabilities.

In addition to benefits, this equation takes into account both the direct and indirect costs of technology, including:

1. The initial purchase costs of the technology (hardware, telecommunications/network purchases; software licensing fees; training costs).
2. The ongoing annual operating costs for the technology (annual maintenance, service).
3. Time value of money (cost of funds). Particularly if the investment requires large capital expenditures, the organization should perform discounted cash flow or lost interest income analysis studies.
4. The number of years the organization expects to utilize the technology (or the number of years to break even or positive returns, as determined from the ROI model).

Investment Approaches

An aggressive approach to benefits quantification and maximization, combined with a focused, dedicated implementation commitment, will yield positive results and economic value. A casual, "if it happens" management approach most likely will result in uncertain or no positive results and economic value. However, benefits need not be purely economic: Although strategic positioning benefits are more difficult to quantify, they may provide a greater eventual return or value for an organization's investment.

Benefits returned from an IT investment may be termed either *incremental* or *breakthrough*. For most organizations today, IT investments focus on incremental benefit returns—those that add simple or moderate value to current work and patient care processes. Some organizations are able to achieve more fundamental, breakthrough returns, engineering completely new and more efficient methods of executing work and patient care processes.

The Incremental Approach

Organizations choosing to adopt an incremental approach to IT investment make low or moderate risk investments to gain equivalent cash or efficiency gains. This approach does not mean the organization takes a relaxed view toward investing or benefits realization; organizations successfully using this approach are just as focused on benefits and ROI as those opting for breakthrough.

Typically, incremental organizations share one or more of the following characteristics:

- Uncertain, or endangered financial position
- A low tolerance for risk (either because of shaky finances or executive mind-set)

- Large, existing financial commitment to information systems (IS) that must be preserved
- Inflexible in-place or existing information systems with little ability to support new organization or work flow designs

In one way or another, all organizations occasionally take an incremental investment approach. Incremental investments might include purchasing an automated scheduling system to handle increased patient volume or implementing a nursing system to cut down on nursing overtime. In both cases, the organization gains direct cash or efficiency benefits, though they normally are of a small or moderate magnitude.

The Breakthrough Approach

Breakthrough thinking requires a fundamental commitment from all levels of the organization to a number of precepts, including:

- The vision to engineer or design completely new service delivery or administrative management processes
- An organization culture of innovation
- Continuous reassessment of goals and priorities throughout the organization
- A willingness to change when reassessment indicates the need
- The desire to "push the envelope" of traditional thinking
- Tolerance for risk, with learning "failures" expected and accepted

Although every organization has within it the *capacity* to reach and implement breakthrough engineering, only a limited number of organizations ever do. A fundamental uneasiness accompanies the breakthrough mentality—a constant, insatiable desire to find "the best," which tends to upset complacency.

For those organizations that do make the breakthrough commitment, the rewards can be tremendous. In this time of market uncertainty, organizations that productively strategize for IT use and maximum ROI will find their influence, survivability, and market position increasing exponentially in a number of ways, including:

- Assumption of a leadership role, sharing their "vision" with other health care organizations and the overall community
- Increased public perception of organizational quality and efficiency
- Increased efficiency in care delivery, resulting in margin improvement
- Better strategic positioning to cope with or drive changes in the health care industry

Controlling Factors

Organizations planning for either incremental or breakthrough returns must evaluate their internal and external environments. There are numerous factors that influence investment return expectations. For example, the disposition and attitude of the decision-making team can change the level of expected or achieved benefits return. Some professionals, as a matter of course, demand greater returns from their investments. The controlling factors that exert the greatest influence on ROI are:

- Location on the IT investment continuum
- Management risk disposition
- Market position
- Financial stability

Location on the IT Investment Continuum

The *IT investment continuum* refers to the general investment cycle that organizations typically experience after a large IT purchase. The point at which an organization resides along this continuum is a key indicator of the importance of current IT investments, as well as the potential flexibility for new investments. A *flexible* organization considers current IT investments largely expendable — old, with already sunk costs — even if they are fairly effective in solving today's requirements. In rare cases, an organization may force flexibility by exhibiting a willingness to "start over," writing off current investments to free up time, finances, and energy in order to build a new IT infrastructure. On the other hand, an *inflexible* organization must preserve its current IT infrastructure to a great extent, even if it is not effective at meeting today's requirements. Reasons abound but usually are associated with board visibility, invested management decisions, or the financial status of the organization. Although certain areas may be more flexible than others (the organizational financial systems may be older, ready to be replaced, whereas clinical systems are newer), this type of organization invests more cautiously in technology.

It is generally true that the older an organization's current investment, the more flexibility there will be in current planning efforts — and the greater the potential to achieve breakthrough ROI economics from newer technologies.

Management Risk Disposition

Unlike positioning in the IT investment continuum, which is dependent upon investment history, management risk disposition depends entirely on human factors and management style. The level of risk that management is willing to support reflects how well positioned the organization may be to invest in IT breakthrough ROI strategies, which often require less-proven, riskier technologies and software suppliers. Although structural factors may determine risk disposition, it is also always a function of the executive team's orientation toward risk and reward.

It is important to note that the greatest risk from IT often lies with the organizational change necessary for implementation. Many technologies fail not because the technology itself is somehow flawed but, rather, because the implementation effort failed to overcome internal resistance to change.

Organizations willing to accept only low levels of risk share a number of characteristics, including one or more of the following:

- A low internal tolerance for change
- A weak market position
- A survival financial position
- A history of unsuccessful IS projects (whether because of poor planning, implementation, or other contributing factors)

Organizations willing to accept high levels of risk also share characteristics, including one or more of the following:

- A strong market position
- Risk-oriented leadership
- A strong financial position
- A perception of IT as a prerequisite to survival, despite the presence of the low-risk indicators above
- A history of successful IS projects

Market Position and Financial Stability

The two other key driving factors in determining an organization's ROI orientation are market position and financial stability. Realistically, given the capital intensity of IT investments, organizations struggling for immediate survival have little room to maneuver when making IT decisions.

These four key indicators—location on the IT investment continuum, management risk disposition, organizational market position, and financial stability—combine into a guiding mosaic that executive teams can use in determining realistic return expectations. Table 1-1 maps these indicators into a grid for choosing incremental versus breakthrough ROI strategies.

Investment Return Cycles

Whatever investment approach organizations choose to pursue—incremental, breakthrough, or a combination of the two—initial returns will be outweighed

Table 1-1.   ROI Decision Spectrum

	Seek Incremental ROI	**Seek Breakthrough ROI**
IT investment continuum	New technology largely installed Highly visible recent expenditures	Old IT Sunk costs viewpoint Modernization of investment required
Management risk disposition	Low tolerance for change or risk	Bold; risk-oriented leadership
Organizational market position	Established niche -or- Aligned with a secure, major partner	Strong: Hold a major position in integrated health delivery (want to solidify or consolidate market) -or- Weak: Require breakthrough strategy
Financial stability	Low: Cash/balance sheet weak; earnings stable or declining	Medium/high: Cash/balance sheet strong; strong, stable, or increasing earnings

by investment costs. Breakthrough investment, particularly, requires a longer cycle before returns manifest, perhaps even twice as long as an incremental investment.

As illustrated in figure 1-2, ROI cycles for incremental and breakthrough projects may vary dramatically. With any new investment comes an initial period of capital and operational outlay, a time when the organization has committed financial and staff resources but has yet to receive any clear benefit from the investment.

Over time, the balance begins to shift, as costs are reduced and stabilized and benefit returns begin to manifest. At one point in the investment cycle, cumulative benefits will equal cumulative costs—the "break-even" point. Particularly with breakthrough investments, most or even all of the initial investment may be expended before even reaching an annual break-even point.

As investment returns begin to amplify, the ROI cycle provides for a period of positive returns for the organization. How steep the return line becomes is driven by the potential of the investment. Incremental investments, designed by nature to provide small or moderate gains in money, time, or resources, will slope more gently than breakthrough investments (those geared to provide strong, continuing returns to the organization). A major new investment, such as a completely new health care information system (HIS), may cycle somewhere between incremental and breakthrough. In evaluating ROI, as the line of returns begins to flatten, organizations should reevaluate, modify, or restructure the investment to prolong and extend positive returns into an annuity stream.

Figure 1-2. Cycles for ROI*

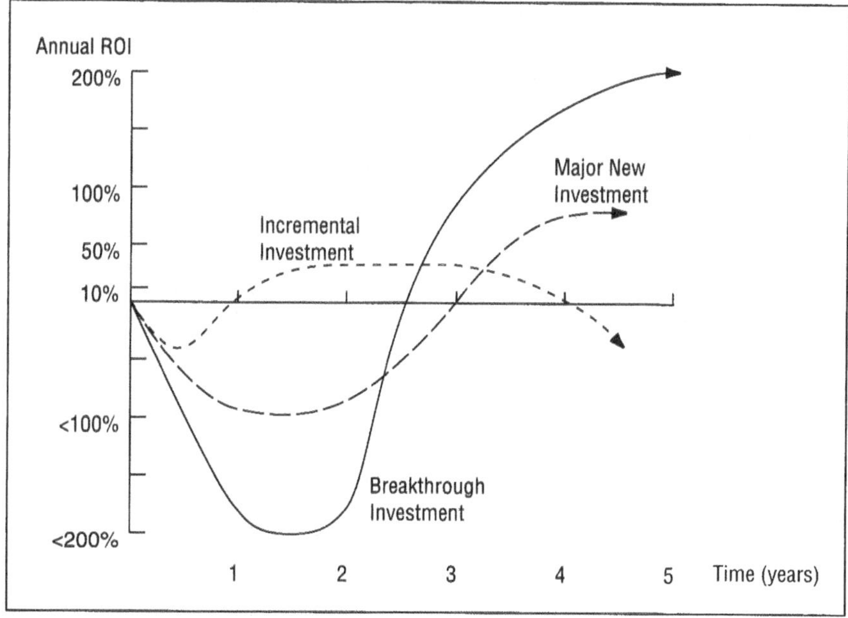

*Conceptual illustration. Returns will vary by project.

IT investments vary in size and complexity, as do their associated returns. Investments may be straightforward, such as the purchasing of a new accounts payable system. They may also be quite complex, such as using IT as a core component of a newly engineered patient delivery system or for inpatient clinical process standardization. Either type of investment, executed well, would show a return over five years; yet the breakthrough engineering strategy would reap far greater returns, perhaps 100 percent or more of the initial investment. Figure 1-3 illustrates theoretical returns for eight IT investments.

Formulating Investment Principles and Guidelines

Taken together, the IT investment continuum and management's risk disposition form the basic quadrants of a strategic benefits orientation model. Illustrated in figure 1-4, the model identifies the four most common approaches health care providers take toward ROI benefits achievement: status quo, minimalist, incremental reengineering, and breakthrough engineering.

In quadrant one, organizations with a low-risk disposition and inflexible IT investments strategize as *status quo.* Technology investment decisions are functional, designed to optimize current investments, and complemented by incremental new investments with low ROI expectations. These organizations typically will avoid extensive automation, waiting until market and business forces clearly demand investment. Investments that are accepted will be those in widespread use across the market (for example, scheduling, admission/discharge/transfer, financials) with numerous stable, proven commercial systems available.

Organizations with a low-risk disposition, but high flexibility in their IT investments generally strategize as *minimalists* (quadrant two). IT decisions are cautious, with investment in technology only after it has been proven by other provider organizations or in other markets. As a rule, emerging technologies are not possibilities for implementation. Potential does exist for ROI "spikes"—through investment in small-scale IT projects with a high ROI potential, such as a managed care contract management system.

Figure 1-3. Theoretical Returns for Several Types of IT Investments*

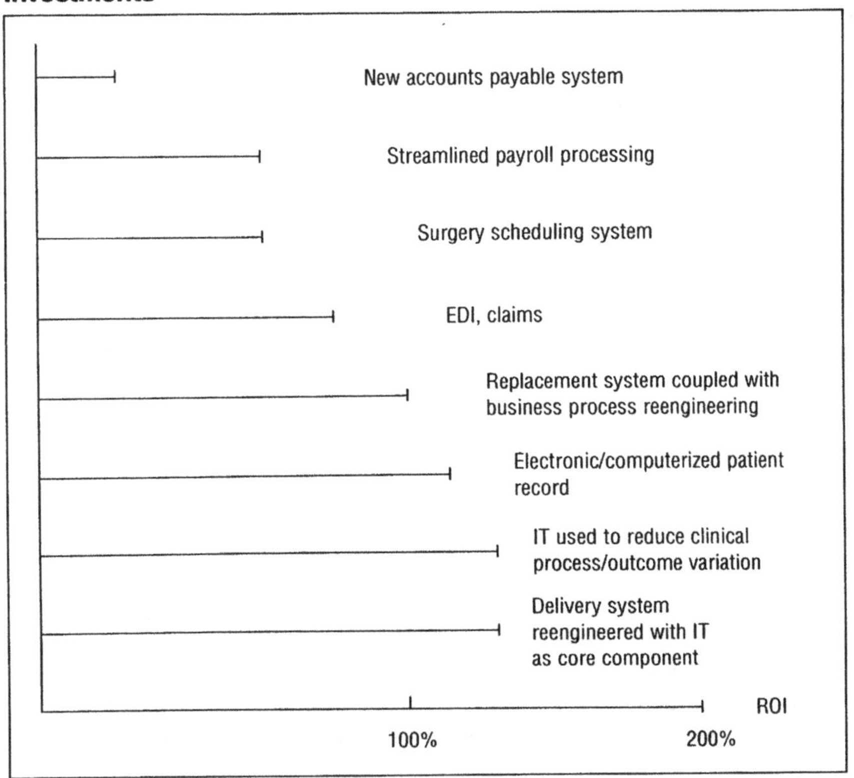

*Returns will vary by project.

Figure 1-4. Strategic Benefits Orientation Model

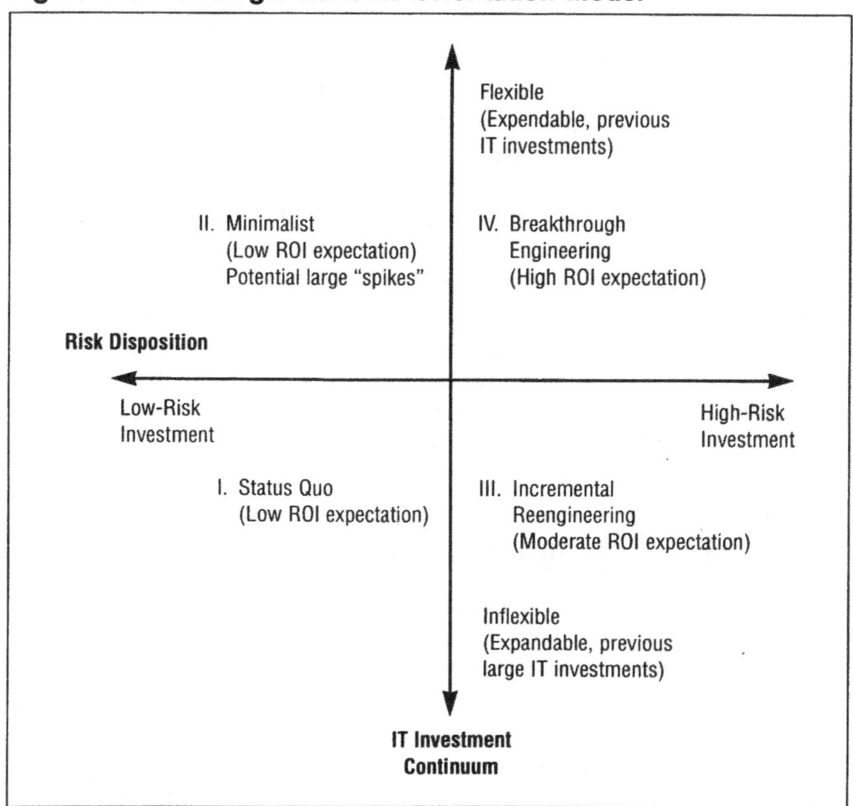

Minimalist and status quo, by their very nature, are closed strategies with little potential for enterprisewide investment return. At best, select incremental returns are possible.

Quadrant three encompasses organizations that are more open to risk taking but also are limited by a lack of flexibility in their IT investments. This type of organization commonly strategizes for *incremental reengineering*—longer-term decisions with greater impact are possible, but implementing them takes careful maintenance and planning. ROI expectations are moderate but based on current IT capabilities. Projects may include small-scale use of handheld prototype systems in the obstetric ward, or redevelopment of existing system profiles to support managed care billing and electronic data interchange (EDI).

Finally, organizations with a great deal of flexibility in IT investments, coupled with a willingness to take risks, fall into quadrant four. These organizations strategize for *breakthrough engineering,* considering IT investments the fulcrum by which they can leverage themselves into the next generation of health care delivery in terms of structure and economics. These organizations may be embarking on the planning and implementation of an enterprisewide electronic medical record (EMR) or clinical data repository (CDR); they may be using multiple technologies and process reengineering efforts to facilitate enterprisewide case management activities.

The strategic benefits orientation model is not intended to be wholly discrete; organizations may exhibit characteristics of multiple categories. For example, an organization with limited flexibility in IT investments may have an executive willing to take risks, "bet the farm" so to speak, thus combining the status quo with incremental reengineering or breakthrough engineering. Similarly, an organization with a great deal of flexibility in IT investments may be unwilling to take the risks necessary for breakthrough engineering, instead choosing to remain minimalist or incremental while preserving a cash-heavy balance sheet.

Choosing a Development Approach

The ability of user application systems to simplify work processes—reducing or eliminating the associated resource requirements—provides the most straightforward business value and specific utility of information technology. Such application systems do not simply appear; rather, they require a conscious manufacturing approach based on human crafting, often referred to as an *IT development process.*

A variety of available IT development options exist, each with distinct advantages, disadvantages, and management and risk consequences to provider organizations. Before selecting an approach, the successful health care provider organization will carefully consider all business and technological implications. The development approach has far-reaching implications in planning and achieving IT-related benefits.

Generally, IT solutions can be categorized as originating from or serving one of the following market segments:

- *Application software/service technologies:* This core group of applications serves the traditional HIS, physician, and managed care markets. Some companies that develop this kind of IT, serving acute care/medical center, physician office, ambulatory, managed care, home health, and decision support market segments, tend to be health care industry specific. Others, offering general financial, payroll, accounts payable, and payroll/ human resource functionalities, tend to cross industries.
- *Original equipment (hardware) technologies:* This marketing segment includes computing equipment and associated devices for data-processing activities and voice-processing (PBX) capabilities. The core companies in

this market tend to be extremely dominant, and to share close links and reseller agreements with application software market vendors.

- *Telecommunications/network service suppliers:* The companies in this marketing segment provide equipment, software, and services to help local, wide, and metropolitan area networks to distribute data capabilities across a wide geographic area.
- *System integration services:* The technical service firms in this segment take responsibility for assembling various application systems and technical networks into a functional IT solution for customers. They also are capable of custom application and data interface development.
- *Community health information network (CHIN) suppliers:* This is a cross-segment view of health care–specific application suppliers, telecommunication suppliers, and public utility telephone companies that view CHINs as an emerging market. This marketing segment is not yet clearly defined from a consumer or supplier perspective.

Development Options

There are two general alternatives for IT development, although several hybrid options exist within each global choice. Provider organizations consider a variety of factors when choosing among IT development options. In deciding whether to purchase packaged software (option 1), custom applications (option 2), or some hybrid of one or both, provider organizations must consider how well situated they are to handle the risks and costs of each alternative. Outside technological and business influences also can drive providers toward one development approach or another.

As illustrated in figure 1-5, providers may either select their information technology from market-available applications — the packaged software

Figure 1-5. IT Development Options

Option	Approaches	Major Dependencies
Packaged software purchase	Critical cluster system architecture (See figure 1-6, p. 16.)	• High-quality application software available on market • Financial strength and delivery capabilities of application company • Underlying technology life cycle
	Single-supplier architecture	
Custom software programming	Internal resource driven	• Underlying technology life cycle • Available personnel and skill set • Management process
	Outsource using systems integration firm	• Financial strength and resource capabilities of systems integration firm

purchase option—or utilize their own resources and talent to specially develop applications—custom software programming—which often allows organizations to better meet their unique IT needs and goals.

The major ROI implications of the two development approaches are presented in table 1-2. These implications can best be summarized in terms of cost predictability, benefit (return) maximization, and investment duration, or life cycle.

This section discusses the basic concepts behind each IT development approach, the typical resource (time, cost) commitments necessary to utilize the approach, the advantages or disadvantages of each alternative, and the potential ROI each option holds for the organization.

Table 1-2. ROI Implications of Development Approaches

	Investment Cost	**Return Potential**	**Life Cycle**
Packaged software purchase	• Can predict costs within acceptable, low margin of error (especially for single-supplier option) • Maintenance costs in order of 70% of purchase costs over five years (12%/year) • Low opportunity cost; can implement on expedient basis	• Benefits must be *optimized* between application features as provided by supplier and specific utility value desired	• Limited by supplier enhancement program and performance • Generally 5+ years • A continuous software upgrade program can extend to 10+ years • Obsolescence most likely will result from a change in business requirements versus a technology requirement
Custom software programming	• Most difficult to predict and control • Maintenance costs, especially to remain current on underlying technology, can exceed development cost by 200% over five years • Longer development cycle can increase opportunity cost	• Benefits can be *maximized* as application features can be customized for provider-specific utility value	• Limited by obsolescence in underlying technology • Generally 3 to 5 years without continued investment

The Packaged Software Option

The health care IT market has evolved into a multibillion dollar industry. Various estimates place annual revenues from as low as $2.8 billion to as high as $7.5 billion.[2] These compiled figures rarely even attempt to account for the purchase of technology from non–health care–specific vendors supporting global business and telecommunications markets.

The life cycle of packaged software systems is threatened by three primary causes of investment obsolescence: supplier insolvency, product line discontinuation, and changing business/medical service requirements. For example, a provider organization may make an investment in a laboratory information system to support an acute care facility and minor outpatient services. A year or two into the life cycle, an integrated delivery system (IDS) may form, and laboratory test-processing requirements may now include multientity as well as site-specific "stat" processing, physician office test processing on a commercial basis, and remote inquiry into lab results across all entities in the delivery system.

These new requirements most likely would require a new system implementation and design, and result in a premature shortening of the current systems investment life cycle. Under normal circumstances, however, the life cycle of a technology can be extended by contracting for maintenance, enhancement, and new release services from the software supplier. This will provide current, up-to-date technology through new and modified system features. Often this type of system update provides an opportunity to seek further ROI, forcing incremental returns based on new releases. A continuous quality improvement (CQI) program surrounding the new release implementation will ensure a continued incremental ROI achievement program. There are two current architectural strategies associated with packaged software development: critical cluster and single supplier.

Critical Cluster Architecture

The first architectural strategy, critical cluster, is illustrated in figure 1-6. A critical cluster architecture allows a logical grouping of database and end-user requirements to form a solution for a business or medical service function or set of functions. By definition, a cluster must be supported by a single software provider operating on a uniform hardware platform. The sole-supplier architecture, by contrast, represents the classic "single-supplier" solution, in which a provider buys 99 percent of all applications from a single health care–specific software supplier.

It is important not to confuse the critical cluster concept with "best-of-breed" architecture, popular during the early to mid-1980s. Under the best-of-breed approach, a cluster (as it would be called today) was broken down into separate application packages that were then purchased from separate

Figure 1-6. Critical Cluster System Architecture

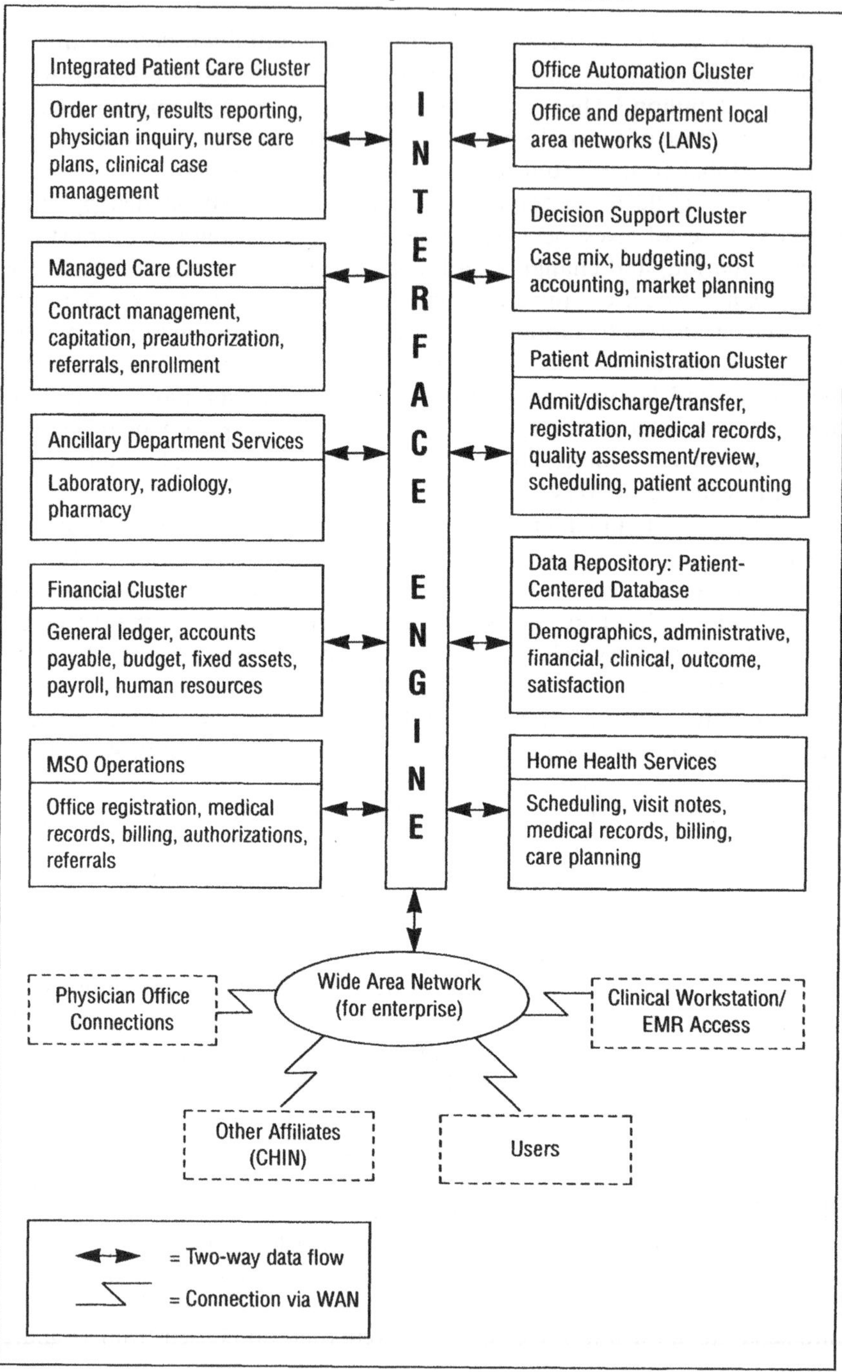

software suppliers. A provider could, in the end, have 30 or more major packaged software suppliers under a best-of-breed approach. Using a critical cluster architecture, the number of suppliers more likely will be three to seven, depending on organizational complexity. More important, under a cluster approach the overall design supports logical data sharing between clusters and very strong user–database integration within a cluster.

To fully optimize the critical cluster approach, provider organizations must develop the interfaces necessary to exchange appropriate data between clusters. However, data-exchange requirements are minimized by the structural design of clusters, because the overwhelming majority of the data required to support a particular business or medical service function reside on a particular cluster.

Current data-exchange standards, such as Health Level 7 (HL7) and the American National Standards Institute (ANSI) set, further facilitate the ease of data exchange and can reduce interface development costs. Providers selecting the critical cluster approach can contract with outside suppliers (for example, interface engine suppliers, application software suppliers, or systems integration firms) to provide interface programming services.

Single-Supplier Architecture

In the single-supplier architecture, providers place complete responsibility for application systems on one health care software supplier. That supplier has responsibility for all systems integration requirements, features development, system and technology updates, and keeping up with market-based requirements. Often the single-supplier architecture will be a cluster architecture from a technical perspective, with the supplier responsible for assembling all application systems into a common presentation such that the end users believe they are using only one technical system.

Packaged Software ROI Potential

As a development approach, selection of commercially available software offers several advantages over custom programming. These advantages are largely associated with the predictability of development costs and the probability that the system actually will be implemented successfully. Packaged software system costs, largely controlled through the acquisition contract, can be predefined with appropriate contingency dollars. Increasingly, technology suppliers will commit to fixed-price contracting for other services (such as interfaces, custom features, installation support), allowing the health care provider to better identify and control costs. Finally, commercial systems, unlike custom-developed ones, generally are proven in one or more health care environments — purchasers can be reasonably certain the system offers adequate functionality for an operational setting.

Benefits achievement with commercial systems will be driven by the available features, functionalities, and adaptation capabilities. Increasingly, systems are provided with advanced "tool sets," allowing provider organizations to support changing business/medical service requirements by adapting, adding, or modifying capabilities without actually changing system programming.

In determining the likelihood of incremental versus breakthrough returns, it is important to consider the organization's situation before the automation project began. An organization implementing automated systems in key areas for the first time often will achieve breakthrough returns by using packaged software, whereas those implementing a new system in an area previously automated might reach only incremental benefit levels. Organizations combining new systems (such as uniform, enterprisewide patient/enrollee registration capabilities) with process or business restructuring (such as a newly formed IDS) also may achieve breakthrough economics.

The Custom Software Option

Custom software programming was the development option of choice during the 1970s and early 1980s. At that time, the health care technology supplier marketplace was emerging and largely based on 1960s technology. Options were limited to either inflexible shared processing systems and/or custom programming. Consequently, automation was limited primarily to basic business and patient finance applications — core business support functions. Patient care automation was limited to large facilities, medical practices, and academic medical centers.

State of the Art

Custom software programming requires that the developing organization take direct responsibility for the creation and support of IT capabilities and applications. Today, custom programming remains a technically viable option. Using development technologies available from the non–health care–specific industry, such as object-oriented programming systems (Object C++), database systems (Sybase, Oracle, Informix, DB2), and application coding systems (COBOL), the custom developers design, program, debug, test, implement, and support application systems. In essence, a provider selecting this development approach also is the software supplier, "manufacturing" a unique system.

Advanced technical tool sets, such as object-oriented programming systems, actually have reduced certain risk factors associated with custom development, such as long development cycles. Custom software development continues to be necessary for certain levels of intrasystem data exchange (although the use of interface engine technology is reducing this need) and for development of unique database and management reporting systems.

The broad availability of commercially available supplier-created and supported applications has clearly, and significantly, reduced the need for and scope of custom software programming. In addition, numerous potential disadvantages deter many organizations from attempting custom development. For example, custom development requires that an organization maintain highly skilled information services staff to provide both technical support for the system and ongoing development of new features and functionalities.

Custom Software ROI Potential

In an ideal world, the custom software programming approach truly can provide the greatest return potential for an organization. The designers of the system, whether staff or contractors, can work with users and management personnel to design an IT solution without preconceived constraints relative to features, functions, and capabilities. A "clean sheet" design can be engineered. At least in theory, breakthrough economic gains can best be supported by a custom software development approach, matching technology to the most efficient business or medical service process for a particular organization. However, the advantage of customization, and the potential high economic return associated with it, generally is limited by two serious disadvantages: cost and time (scheduling) commitments.

The cost of a custom development cycle is very difficult to predict or control. Because the system does not yet exist when decision makers review the economic feasibility, approximations must be made—approximations historically low, relative to actual development costs. It is not uncommon for development costs to exceed original estimates by a factor of two to three times.

The time frame needed to design and implement custom systems can be long, resulting in a need to redesign features constantly (adding cost), as well as delaying the start of the return component of the investment cycle. These factors make it wise to carefully study custom development proposals and explore hidden assumptions for realism.

Often a sensitivity simulation can be performed to determine the impact of cost overages or a delay in (or nonachievement of) benefits on overall ROI calculations. This type of simulation is an important tool in managing custom development projects, holding the project team accountable for meeting (or explaining variance in not meeting) clearly defined goals, objectives, and benefit targets. Through a clear-headed examination of project progress, decision makers can evaluate the ongoing potential that desired ROI will be achieved, considering project progress, levels of investment, and outside risk factors (including technical, IS personnel/contractor performance).

Regardless of the disadvantages, in some circumstances organizations stand to benefit from the use of custom-developed solutions. Custom development most commonly occurs in immature application markets (today, the clinical workstation and EMR IS markets are hotbeds of custom development activity). Providers with strong relationships with application vendors/developers may choose to invest resources in a partnership, accepting shared risk for development influences and potential financial returns.

Key Factors Influencing Development

As discussed earlier in this chapter, an organization's place on the ROI decision spectrum—incorporating its position on the investment continuum, management risk disposition, organizational market position, and financial stability—should provide the driving motivation for all IT investment decisions. However, other key influences on development approaches are the systems life cycle and the changing business and medical information requirements. An analysis of these factors can pinpoint, with relative accuracy, the approach to IT investment an organization should take.

The Systems Life Cycle

Similar to other capital equipment or physical plant investment-based life cycles, IT investments behave cyclically. Initially, costs realize a high rate of return—utility—over time, but to extend this return, the investment requires continued upgrades and maintenance. Eventually, the investment becomes obsolescent from either a technological or business practice viewpoint. At this point, a new investment is required to receive maximum operational value for the organization.

The process through which an investment is planned, selected (or developed), implemented, utilized, and reevaluated is typically referred to as the *IT systems life cycle.* Activities within the life cycle are geared to optimize and retain the highest rate of return for the investment for the longest period of time.

Figure 1-7 illustrates a management view of the health care IS life cycle. The investment life cycle generally begins with the completion or modernization of an IT long-range plan (LRP), which defines numerous central management and technical parameters for the organization. Although the step-by-step process of conducting an LRP is beyond the scope of this book,[3] a summary LRP is presented in chapter 4 as a model.

Through the long-range planning process, a number of critical activities and decisions are performed and operationalized, relating to three areas of importance:

1. Planning
2. Technology selection and/or development
3. Implementation and operations

Planning

Through the course of long-range IT planning, strategic decisions are made on a number of levels relating to investment guidelines, principles, budgets, and action plans.

1. The decision to "expend" or "expand" current IT investments (described earlier as a critical parameter in determining ROI expectations) must be analyzed in detail, and a position determined.

2. The optimum desired length of the investment (typically three to five years for IT-based investments) must be determined, with strategies formulated for maximizing the investment's practical life cycle.
3. The overall development approach (custom versus purchase) must be selected to facilitate benefits planning and fundamental decisions regarding architectural structure.

Technology Selection and/or Development

Upon completion of planning activities, provider organizations must begin a series of overlapping activities designed to implement the IT plan successfully.

1. Quantify and further develop benefits expectations associated with the chosen IT strategy and specific investment approaches.
2. Establish and maintain user activities consistent with global business goals.
3. Prepare for actual implementation of the new technology. When planning the change from one system to another (system cutover), it is important to plan for benefits achievement through concurrently implementing new procedures, policies, and practices. This forces users to break old habits and positions the organization to move forward.
4. Build or buy the software system.

Figure 1-7. IS Life Cycle

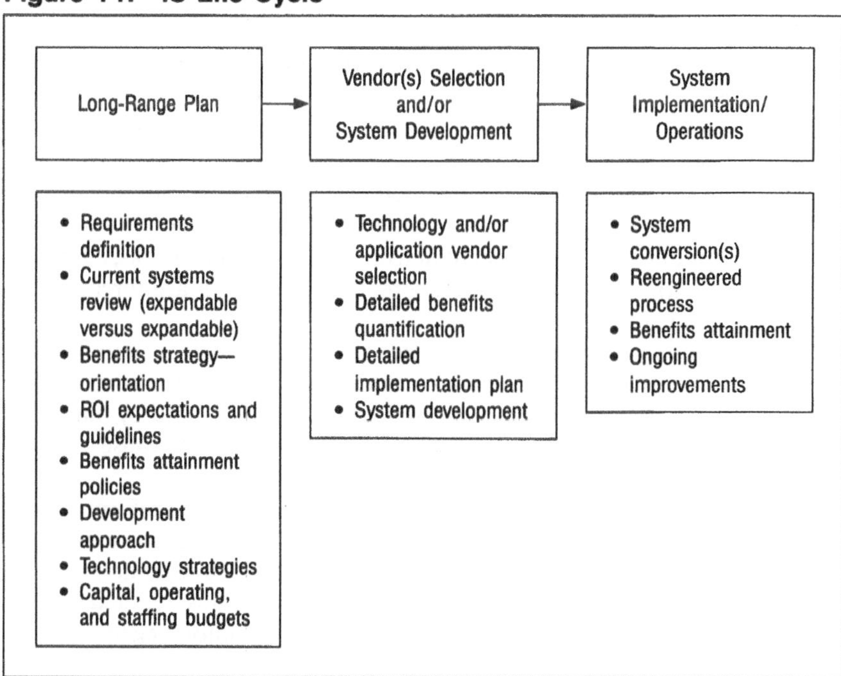

Implementation and Operations

The systems implementation and operations phase is the period when users convert to, or begin use of, new IT capabilities and systems. This phase lends itself to simultaneous CQI efforts to further enhance use of new technology and achieve greater return on the IT investment. Ongoing measurement, maintenance, and improvement of IT capabilities should be performed to ensure both IT/business/medical service harmony and up-to-date technology.

Changing Business and Medical Information Requirements

As the emphasis of health care continues to move away from inpatient, acute care facilities, the administrative and clinical complexities of delivering health care increase exponentially. Cost containment pressures from insurers, the government, and the public force providers to maintain the quality of health care, reduce the cost of providing it, and provide increasingly accurate documentation and measurement of both cost and quality.

As business and medical information requirements continue to change, technology suppliers must adjust both the availability and functionality of technology to meet those needs. Four changes having particular impact on the development of new and expanded health care information technology are:

1. *The maturing provider market:* The current level of market penetration has placed increasing influence in the hands of provider organizations. Today's vendors must be more responsive to development requests and the overall desires of health care organizations. Product emphasis has broadened, with new attention to emerging markets, as technology suppliers attempt to capture new markets and make incremental gains in existing ones.
2. *Changing provider delivery models:* Clinically and geographically diverse groups of providers continue to come together to support a complete continuum of care. As the potential technology market shrinks, suppliers are faced with larger risk/reward potentials and again are forced to be more responsive to providers.
3. *The continuing growth of managed care:* As increasing numbers of Americans enroll in managed care health plans, the IS requirements for these plans will increase significantly. Delivery shifts caused by managed care, such as capitation, precertification, and authorization, cause changes in the way information is used and accessed.
4. *Increased/changing regulation and reform efforts:* Ongoing reform efforts recognize the importance of clinical and other information in evaluating the process of care. Successful IT suppliers must have proactive plans for monitoring and implementing changes and programs initiated by federal, state, and local governments, as well as regulatory agencies.

Building a Framework

Whatever controlling factors they face, health care organizations are not inextricably locked into any one approach to ROI. Often the most successful organizations adopt a mixture of approaches, making moderate investments in low-priority areas while taking on sensible, but larger, risks in others. In all cases, however, organizations should have a clear understanding of the situational and environmental characteristics driving their need to invest in information technology. That understanding, coupled with a clear look at the alternative ways in which they can build an IT framework, is critical in successfully and productively meeting an organization's needs and ensuring an ROI that is acceptable to the organization.

Notes

1. *The CEO's Guide to Health Care Information Systems* (Joseph M. DeLuca, with Rebecca Enmark Cagan, Chicago: AHPI, 1996) provides a more in-depth look at the steps involved in the long-range planning process.

2. A cautionary note about existing industry measurements: Compilation methods and inclusiveness vary. Some use annual sales figures of application software/ service suppliers, others include related hospital expenditures (products and services associated with IT purchases, including consulting assistance in selection and implementation).

3. *The CEO's Guide to Health Care Information Systems* (Joseph M. DeLuca, with Rebecca Enmark Cagan, Chicago: AHA, 1996) and *Health Care Information Systems: An Executive's Guide for Successful Management* (Joseph M. DeLuca, with Owen Doyle, Chicago: AHPI, 1991) both cover the long-range planning process in detail.

Realistic Return on Investment: Achievable Benefits of Information Technology

Information technology (IT) comes with no inherent guarantee of realizing benefits. Just as well-planned IT strategy and execution can catapult a health care organization into industry leadership, poorly planned or poorly executed IT investments can cause irreparable harm. Long-range IT planning must incorporate a benefits philosophy and associated IT development strategy with realistic benefits expectations. Those expectations, tied to organizational goals, ensure that the IT focus aligns with the larger organization's mission and direction.

Executive decision makers typically formulate benefits expectations from a number of sources, including past personal experience with a technology, established industry sources, or simply a logical "fit" between a particular activity and a technology. However, specific features and capabilities of technology only partially drive the likelihood of positive return on investment (ROI); numerous organizational characteristics also affect successful benefits achievement.

This chapter discusses how those characteristics, organizational strategy, and technological capabilities combine to form an articulated, realistic assessment of ROI for a provider organization. Specific discussion topics include:

- Matching technology features with expected IT benefits
- Organization and market-specific characteristics that affect benefits achievement
- Macro-level benefits of technology
- Micro-level (functional) benefits of technology

Throughout the latter half of the chapter, discussion focuses on the concrete costs and benefits of technology. This type-by-type discussion of technology presents actual benefits that health care organizations have reported from IT implementation or use. Benefits experiences are drawn from JDA consulting engagements as well as readily available industry data. Technologies surveyed include: networking and telecommunications; electronic data interchange (EDI); and health care information systems, including general financial systems, patient financial and administrative systems, decision support systems, managed care systems, clinical systems, and ancillary department systems.

The chapter focuses on IT features (such as user data access and reporting techniques) as well as functionality — specific capabilities of an IT application, such as production of an HCFA (Health Care Financing Administration) 1500 billing form. Often these similar concepts are used interchangeably.

Evaluating the Potential of Information Technology

Automating a badly run or inefficient process only yields an automated badly run or inefficient process. Organizations investing in any technology should reexamine, redefine, or even rebuild work flow and procedures to optimize its potential. IT investments that combine functionality with such process improvement, redesign, or reengineering efforts provide the greatest potential for ROI.

Organizations must consider more than the features and functionalities available from a technology in evaluating its ROI and benefits potential. Features and functions will drive a certain base level of return, but the true utility of an investment comes when organizational and strategic requirements are aligned with it.

Establishing and managing realistic, harmonious objectives among those involved in an IT investment (for example, management, different user groups) is important to the investment's ultimate success. Often the impact and importance of potential benefits will have different weights among different users. Aligning overall expectations at the highest possible decision-making level is critical. A 1994 study[1] compared nursing staff evaluations of the most important information systems (IS) benefits against those of the general hospital staff. Only *one* benefit made the top five lists of both groups. This is typical of organizations that conduct decentralized or uncoordinated IT projects.

The strategic benefits orientation (discussed in chapter 1), whether geared toward *incremental* or *breakthrough* returns, drives the extent and scope of the IT investment. (For example, an organization considering an investment in a nursing IS with care planning functionality would, based on its strategic benefits orientation, direct implementation and redesign initiatives into different areas. If management is looking for incremental benefits, it may simply use the system to retool existing processes, standardizing certain aspects of care and perhaps reducing staff overtime in the process. On the other hand, if management is looking for breakthrough benefits, it may use care planning as one component of an enterprisewide case management initiative, completely reflowing the clinical care processes associated with nursing staff as well as other clinical providers.

Quantifying Benefit Expectations

In the early IT planning stages, it may be difficult to fully quantify benefit expectations. However, planning efforts should work toward systematically matching current organizational goals—business and medical—with associated IT implications. This process will bring to light both the benefits an organization should pursue and the technological features most likely to provide those benefits. Organizations using this benefits-based, long-range planning typically secure two strategic planning advantages. First, identifying the IT implications associated with an organization's business and medical goals may help illuminate previously unconsidered goals. For example, a home health component of a regional delivery system may decide to implement a computer-based care documentation system using personal digital assistants (PDAs) over a cellular network. After a review of the favorable efficiencies, the health system may consider a new goal of gaining similar efficiencies in ambulatory care centers by adopting the same technology.

Second, the organization will be able to see which of its business objectives can be easily reached in tandem with the IT use. For example, a goal to reduce accounts receivable levels by 20 percent may be driven by the use of EDI technologies such as electronic claims and remittance processing. Implementing this technology also facilitates the organization's ability to accept and manage capitated or other managed care contracts. Detailed benefits and features planning allows the organization to identify ITs that support multiple organizational objectives—a persuasive methodology for prioritizing and funding IT projects.

Organizational Business and Medical Objectives

Every organizational objective has IT ramifications. Through identifying systems and technology needs, planners can formulate a list of general IT features and associated benefits that support the organizational objective. Table 2-1 shows the progression from a long-term business objective to general IT benefits. This organization has identified a primary business goal—building an integrated delivery system (IDS)—and two key strategies for achievement—a seamless continuity of care and increased physician assimilation into the system. Each of those achievement strategies has clear IT implications which, in turn, generate a list of potential benefits to the organization. Note how multiple achievement strategies increase the list of potential IT benefits.

Organizations can use this same process to identify short-term objectives or to overcome specific organizational problems. As a result, near-term IT projects or initiatives, providing incremental benefit returns, may be developed and implemented.

Table 2-1. From Business Objective to Benefit

Business Objective	Achievement Strategy	IT Implications	Potential Benefits
Transform organization into a regional, integrated delivery system	1. Create a seamless "continuity of care" flow of services for • Primary care • Acute care • Referred care • Home care • Long-term care • Occupational medicine • Rehabilitative care	• Regional master patient index • Clinical service tracking • Case management systems All transcending provider and location	• Greater marketing outreach through use of prior information and preadmission capabilities • Essential patient origin, physician referral, and related statistics available for further research and analysis • Significant decrease in administrative paperwork and preparation
	2. Assimilate and invite primary and secondary physicians into the system	• Physician access network, with clinical and administrative functionality • Ad hoc clinical program management analysis and flexible reporting databases • Comprehensive patient-level planning database, with referral information, patient origins, and outcomes	• Increased convenience for affiliated physicians • Physicians have more time for direct patient care • Real-time access to data speeds ability to make care decisions • Improved quality of clinical data through use of outcomes studies • Increased physician awareness and understanding of factors affecting profitability and referral

The Feature–Benefit Connection

Features and functionalities of technology often are mistaken for benefits. Many organizations place tremendous emphasis on selecting an IS with the greatest functionality, forgetting that those features may not actually translate to specific benefits for the organization. IT features and functionalities must be present to achieve benefits but are not, in and of themselves, wholly adequate selection criteria. Provider organizations must consciously plan how to use features and functions to achieve benefits, instituting work redesign efforts to maximize ROI potential.

Once organizational objectives have been mapped to a list of general IT implications and benefits, providers can begin to comprehensively review both specific benefits and technological features to maximize ROI. As shown in table 2-1, this process can be used to work through IT planning from organizational objectives to potential benefits. It also is possible to reverse this process and use it to address a particular organizational need, as illustrated in figure 2-1. Organizations considering less-established technologies or involved in custom software programming may find such reversal particularly helpful in estimating and minimizing risk. (Chapter 1 introduces the idea of custom programming; chapter 3 covers the provider implications in detail.) Figure 2-1 illustrates the correlation among problems, features, and benefits. (Appendix A similarly details each of the technologies discussed in this chapter.)

Methods for Measuring Benefits

All the effort put into planning a technology's benefits frequently is wasted by organizations that never take time to evaluate the benefits they actually realize. The single most commonly ignored step in the IS life cycle (discussed in chapter 1) is the systematic measurement and evaluation of the IT investment.

Figure 2-1.   Correlation among Problems, Features, and Benefits

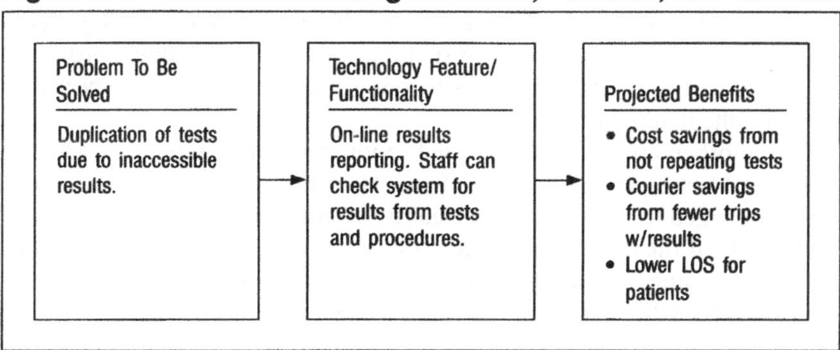

There are a number of techniques that organizations typically use to measure the benefits of technology. Many rely on "eyeball" reviews, although quantified methods — such as time-and-motion studies, flowcharting, work measurement, and repetitive motion-based and limited "human intervention" — may provide more reliable quantifications of economic returns. For example, an organization that implements a system for on-line results reporting to reduce the number of duplicative test orders (as illustrated in figure 2-1) has a number of options through which system benefits could be measured. An eyeball review of the lab could show that technicians are not as busy or that fewer samples are waiting to be tested. To quantify those benefits, the provider organization could study test volume, focusing on the subset of tests that are repeat orders. The organization also might compare average inpatient length of stay (LOS) pre- and postsystem implementation.

This book makes no attempt to judge or validate these measurement methods. Many such methodologies exist, and it is up to the individual training and preferences of the executive team to select one for its organization.

Evaluating Costs and Benefits

Some costs and benefits are not tied specifically to any one type of information technology but, rather, might occur with any type or level of automation. In other cases, IT may act as a fundamental enabler for a large redesign, reengineering, or process improvement effort. Although the project as a whole might well save millions of dollars, attributing those savings to a particular use of technology may be difficult or impossible.

In 1994, when MultiCare Health System (Tacoma, WA) initiated an organizational redesign, it relied heavily on information systems. The key emphases of the new system were high user availability, database repositories, and extendibility for additional functionality. This redesign[2] resulted in a number of benefits to staff, caregivers, and the organization. Taken as a whole, the project saved $6 million in operating expenses in the 1992–1993 fiscal year, exposed network patients to half as many faces during a care episode, and allowed caregivers to spend more time on the direct provision of care. Attributing these benefits to one single use of technology would be difficult, if not impossible.

In another situation, IT was used to join previously separate organizations. In Minnesota, when HealthSpan Health Systems Corporation and Medica merged to become Allina Health System, "information" was identified as one of the three major vision focuses of the new organization. With a $45 million annual budget, the IS department developed seven key achievement strategies to tie the new $2 billion enterprise together.[3]

High-Level Benefits of Technology

The implementation and use of technology has been tied to any number of organizational benefits. Whether quantified, nonquantified, or simply strategic, those benefits typically will accomplish one of three things for an organization:

1. They will reduce costs or increase revenues.
2. They will improve or help to maintain quality.
3. They will improve or enhance work processes.

Reduced Cost/Increased Revenue

In a 1994 survey, 66 percent of respondents said they had an IS-based cost-control strategy.[4] Quantified studies of IT benefits focus in on cost, media, and labor or time savings. For example, the compact storage capabilities of most computer systems allow storage of more data in smaller spaces, reducing paper, microfilm, and microfiche costs, as well as freeing up physical storage space. Additionally associated with that reduction is a saving in supply and labor costs and a positive impact on the environment.

Improved/Maintained Quality

Automating work processes often allows facilities to handle large or increased volumes of patients without adding staff. Automation also can reduce labor and time requirements to perform necessary duties. For example, an automated voice mail system can efficiently route a larger volume of calls than a human telephone operator; manual reporting processes may become incredibly simple through the ability of an ad hoc report writer attached to a master database. Cost savings through reduced staffing needs often also are cited as a major benefit of technology—breakthrough organizations redirect that labor to a more direct focus on the mission and goals of the organization.

Improved or Enhanced Work Processes

IT selection and implementation requires a great deal of focus and planning. Throughout the course of this planning, organizations have a rare chance to examine the process by which they do business. Promoted effectively, an automation project becomes an opportunity to find ways to perform tasks faster, more efficiently, or with less frustration.

The underlying logic of technology forces consistency on users: The structure of a database is the same when entering patient #10000 as it was when patient #1 was input. As record keeping becomes more structured, the organization's ability to make global studies or implement wide-scale changes improves. On a broader scale, the reduced number of "lost" or "unavailable" charts, files, records, messages, and so on improves the likelihood that staff members will be able to gain access to necessary information in a timely fashion. Table 2-2 illustrates a whole range of benefits generally available from IT.

Typical Costs of Technology

The hard-dollar and human costs of implementing IT vary by organization; some, already well prepared to make the leap to a new or improved technology, will pay very little. These organizations typically have a well-thought-out IT program, with a current long-range plan and a strong organizational executive (for example, a chief information officer). Existing systems are kept current, with new releases and technologies integrated on a regular basis. Networking and telecommunications technologies—key backbones of any IT program—are clearly laid out, with enterprisewide

Table 2-2.   General Benefits of Automation

Process	Quality	Cost
• Can promote positive organizational change through work flow redesign, reduced unnecessary administrative burden • Key support tool for reengineering initiatives • Promotes process clarification and analysis	• Reduced problems from illegible handwriting • Less need for redundant record keeping; reduced potential for data errors • More consistent capture of required data elements • Reduced number of "lost"/"unavailable" physical records • Single point of access (terminal, telephone) improves user ability to find necessary information • Consistent record structures improve user chance of finding required data • Simplified access across geographically diverse locations, points of care	• Economic savings (for example, reduces need for paper, microfilm, microfiche; saves on storage space requirements) • Staff time savings (purchasing, inventory, distribution) • Environmental savings

availability. Other organizations, not so well prepared, may have to spend significant sums on infrastructure upgrades (telecommunications, networks, existing application systems) to bring the organization to a point where it can even consider a particular IT investment. (See table 2-3 for a breakdown of the general capital and operational costs of IT investment.)

In addition to capital and operational costs, information technology can generate some strategic costs that organizations should be aware of before they invest. Selecting an overall strategy and prioritizing investment goals by necessity implies that other areas or technologies will not be utilized. Limited investment dollars must be focused on areas where they have the potential to return the most benefits. In addition, once an automation strategy has been selected, other considerations emerge that must be addressed, such as data security, data formatting, and standardization. In an industry where consolidation and collaboration between and across entities is becoming increasingly common, dealing proactively with these issues is critical. As providers merge or are acquired, or become participants in

Table 2-3.   Capital and Operational Cost Considerations

Cost	Capital	Operational
Hardware (purchasing new equipment, bringing old equipment up to required standards)	✔	
Application and operating system software	✔	
Telecommunications (cabling, comm. lines, hubs, routers)	✔	✔
Establishing/remodeling facility to maintain equipment	✔	
Establishing/implementing procedures • Help desk • Backup and recovery • Data confidentiality and security, particularly across diverse providers/locations	(maybe) ✔	✔
Disaster planning, establishing emergency power supply; fire; electric; heating, ventilation, air conditioning (HVAC)	✔	
Peripheral equipment (printers, etc.)	✔	
Ongoing software and hardware maintenance		✔
Training of staff and vendor • Prior to implementation • Ongoing (new and old staff)		✔
Change/stress management • Education— use/purposes/benefits of the system, staff "buy-in" • People costs of reengineering "tradition"		✔

a community health information network (CHIN), the security and compatibility of fundamentally different data sets may generate tremendous costs to organizations.

Benchmarking Benefits Experiences

The technological costs and benefits discussed in this section are drawn directly from provider organization experiences. They have been culled from published case studies, interviews, and consulting engagements. Rather than a detailed case study presentation or an evaluation of any particular vendor's products, this information is presented from a pragmatic viewpoint, with two primary purposes:

1. To examine the realistic possibilities of various information technologies
2. To illustrate what has actually been accomplished by provider organizations through the use of automation

Postimplementation studies measuring benefits have become more and more available, as organizations increasingly recognize the need to share success—and failure—to advance the state of industry practice. For each type of technology, benefits may be directly quantified or nonquantified. Nonquantified investments may be only logically attributed to a technology, strategic in nature, or simply difficult or impossible to quantify. For example, a hospital facility implements an automated series of care protocols with on-line alerts to guide staff in the selection of a diagnosis or treatment. After a period of consistent use of the protocols, it seems logical to assume that staff will become more educated and knowledgeable in various treatments and diagnoses. Such an improvement might be difficult to quantify, let alone tie directly to the use of the protocol system.

A number of factors are important to consider when benchmarking the results of an IT program or initiative:

- The scope of the IT investment or project
- The condition of the organization prior to implementing the technology
- The measurement method used by the organization to gauge the technology benefits

In the vast majority of cases cited here, process improvement, redesign, or reengineering efforts enhanced the ROI of the technology discussed. The groups of technologies discussed in the following subsections include:

- Networking and telecommunications
- Electronic data interchange
- Information systems

Networking and Telecommunications Technologies

Networking and telecommunications technologies allow humans and machines to communicate across geographic distances. Specific technologies in use in the health care environment include local and wide area networks, telephone systems, and interface applications. These technologies are providing critical benefits in a number of areas, including:

- As the continuum of care and longitudinal focus on the patient becomes the standard, the ability to transmit data across information systems is essential for provider organizations.
- As provider organizations continue to grow and consolidate, networking and telecommunications technologies prove key to establishing and maintaining day-to-day operations.

Functional Potential

For the small, single hospital or facility, a local area network (LAN) may provide office automation functionality. Through the LAN, the organization's common applications, such as word processing or electronic mail, can reside in a centralized location rather than be distributed across separate, noncommunicating machines. In larger facilities, with multiple sites, a wide area network (WAN) may allow executive peers in different physical locations to access and review a common enterprise application, such as a decision support system.

With increasing geographic distances between affiliated providers and the growth of telemedical technology, telephone systems and services are more and more critical to provider organizations. "Smart" routers (telephone systems that automatically select the lowest-cost line), automated call processors (voice mail, interactive voice systems), and call-in information systems are just a few of the ways providers are taking advantage of the benefits of this technology.

Interface applications allow disparate systems to communicate data. Through their use, provider organizations can share consistent data across multiple locations and points of service. This functionality supports not only provider consolidation and affiliation, but also several new and emerging technologies including the longitudinal patient record and the CHIN.

Reported Benefits

Organizations using telecommunications and networking technologies have reported cost, process, and quality benefits from project initiatives. To a large extent, the amount and combination of benefits they report depend on the scope of the investment. Typically, benefits (particularly cost savings) come from a variety of small to mid-size improvements.

One common cost benefit reported by provider organizations is a reduction in duplicative data entry. For example, through use of a LAN, the data from patient encounter forms can be uploaded automatically into the billing system, rather than reentered manually. Reducing this redundant effort also limits the number of potential "failure" points from human data entry, increasing the likelihood that data will be accurate and consistent across systems. Accounts receivable may benefit from network technology, as the automated claims submission process is able to bill payers in a more timely fashion. Another potential benefit from network technology is a reduction in the number of claims denied by payers because of incomplete data.

Facilities standardizing on an IT network backbone simplify the maintenance and training demands on IS staff. As organizations grow and change, standard network protocols ease growth, because there are no proprietary schemes to integrate in and maintain. With one global protocol for network systems, when a facility is added or moves, adapting the information systems to the new situation requires fewer resources than would be required working from a mixture of nonstandard systems and equipment.

For the end user, a standard network protocol minimizes the amount of information employees must learn and familiarizes them with equipment located throughout organizational facilities — a particular benefit to organizations with staff moving frequently from one location to another. With standardization across facilities, it becomes much easier for employees to move between physical locations. Data access becomes less tied to one certain machine, and familiar protocols encourage use by technology-shy clinicians.

The Medical Center of Delaware (Wilmington) achieved some impressive economic and efficiency returns after networking five geographically separated sites onto the same technical backbone.[5] In doing so, the center was able to reduce receivables by $40 million in the first year of the investment. Links between patient financial systems and clinical/ancillary systems captured an additional $1 million in charge revenue, and labor requirements were reduced by 13,000 hours annually. Overall, the organization was able to reduce working capital requirements from $1.3 million to less than $400,000.

Telecommunications technology is increasingly being looked at by organizations as a tool to improve service or to maintain service levels without adding staff resources. Kaiser Permanente's Northern California Region (headquartered in Oakland), facing a large volume of patient calls, centralized its appointment system using automated call processors to reduce the number of misdirected calls. At the same time, medical information tapes were automated, saving staff time and ensuring that patients received standardized information.[6]

When Lexington Medical Center, in West Columbia, South Carolina, issued cellular phones to nursing staff during shifts, it found that the nurses spent significantly less time walking back and forth between patient rooms and reception areas. Using the phones, nurses were able to get their next assignment immediately rather than walking back to a central area. Each staff member saved more than 12 hours a week, time staff could then refocus into direct patient care.[7]

Telecommunications technology can be an effective cost-control tool, as well. Automated call routers and processors can diminish the human resources required to maintain service volumes. Mercy Medical Center, in Cedar Rapids, Iowa, turned to a predictive dialer to improve its collections capabilities. The system automatically dials patient numbers, downloading account information for review by a collections specialist. When the phone is answered, patient information is displayed and the staff member alerted. After implementing the system, Mercy reported a 300 percent increase in productivity, with staff members making 900 to 1,700 additional calls per week.[8]

When Rush-Presbyterian-St. Luke's Medical Center, in Chicago, conducted a patient satisfaction survey, staff discovered that noise from the nurse call system intercoms and audible paging system was creating negative patient impressions. In response, the center instituted a wireless voice-call communications system. After two months, there had been a 74 percent decrease in unit intercom pages. After implementing a one-way communication system, which used various vibrations to indicate types of message (such as a phone call), pages decreased 68.5 percent.[9]

The growing popularity of interface engine technology, with its ability to integrate existing application system technologies, has led many provider organizations to consider investing. Alexian Brothers Medical Center, in Elk Grove Village, Illinois, reportedly saved $250,000 from such an investment. By implementing an interface engine, Alexian Brothers was able to avoid the technical and resource costs of developing and maintaining point-to-point interfaces between their information systems. The center achieved additional benefits when it used the capabilities of the interface engine to automatically pull information on small-balance, bad-debt accounts. In doing so, a full-time equivalent (FTE) position was saved in the collections department, allowing staff to focus on higher-balance accounts.[10]

Investment Considerations

Of special concern with any technology that services discontinuous areas (different offices, different buildings, towns, states, and so on) is the security of communications. Maintaining and monitoring the level of access allowed to authorized users and adjusting that access as necessary, particularly in large organizations, is no small task. In one 1994 study,[11] 47 percent of the respondents indicated that the computer access of terminated employees was not removed for more than 24 hours after the fact.

Common throughout computer literature are cases of outsiders "hacking" into computer and telephone networks, causing a variety of mischief to the unlucky targeted organization. A few of the various miseries that could occur from such "hacking" include:

- Computer files may be read or downloaded by unauthorized parties (causing legal as well as operational ramifications).
- Unauthorized toll or long-distance phone charges may accrue to the organization's account.
- A virus may be placed in the system, causing file or system damage.

Continued Growth

As organizations continue to merge and consolidate operations, networking and telecommunications technologies will be an important investment for health care providers. The continued growth in integrated/regional delivery systems (IDS/RDS), as well as numerous CHIN initiatives are indications of the continued advance and utilization in this area.

In addition to IDS, RDS, and CHIN activities, providers are beginning to take advantage of the capabilities offered by the Internet, a mammoth network of networks descended from the Department of Defense's ARPANET (started in 1969). The popularity of the Internet for both research and communications is increasing in health care, although use levels still lag behind those of private industry. Forty-nine percent of the respondents to the 1994 HIMSS/HP survey indicated that their facility was "on" the Internet; in a survey of *Fortune* 1,000 companies conducted by Forrester Research, Inc., the percentage of companies indicating Internet access was much higher, nearly two-thirds.[12] (The uses and potential of the Internet are discussed more fully in chapter 3.)

Electronic Data Interchange

Electronic data interchange (EDI) is the use of computerized systems to conduct transactions associated with daily business operations. According to the Healthcare Information and Management Systems Society (HIMSS), provider organization use of EDI has increased steadily over the past two years. Table 2-4 shows the growth in use in some of the EDI functionalities. According to the same survey, in 1994, fully 36 percent of organizations responding were using EDI to facilitate (at least partially) benefits coordination between multiple payers.

Functional Potential

For health care facilities, EDI technology can be used to conduct a variety of administrative, financial, and materials management activities, including enrollment transactions, eligibility verification, claims submission, payment

Table 2-4.   HIMSS Survey: Use of EDI in 1993 versus 1994

Functionality	1993 % of respondents using EDI	1994 % of respondents using EDI
Claims processing	68	68
Materials management	54	62
Remittance processing	54	59
Managed care certification	26	39

Source: The HIMSS/Hewlett-Packard Leadership Survey, 1993 and 1994.

and remittance, claims inquiry, materials management, prescription ordering, test ordering/results reporting, coordination of benefits, referrals and preauthorizations, remote appointment scheduling, and medical records exchange.

The impact and potentials of EDI on work flow, claims processing, and reimbursement have been studied extensively. Although EDI's full potential in health care has not been fully realized, this application-to-application transfer of standard data sets has a clear and immediate impact on labor time and costs for participating organizations.

Reported Benefits

Quantified benefit studies of EDI generally center on the areas of claims processing and reimbursement, materials management, banking, and home health care. The Workgroup for Electronic Data Interchange (WEDI), a public/private task force established to study and make recommendations for using EDI to reduce health care administrative costs, has reported the potential of enormous industry cost savings through the use of EDI. The WEDI Cost Savings Analysis[13] projected a conservative-case, industrywide savings scenario of nearly $4.5 billion. Some of these cost savings come from increased access and availability of test results leading to fewer redundant tests, reduced courier and paper costs, and reduced LOS for inpatients. Others come from labor savings from standardized information and procedures, increased claims accuracy, and reduced postage, forms, and telephone expenses. The WEDI study also estimated a cumulative $1.6 billion savings through materials management EDI applications for acute care hospitals using a standard interface. According to the study, using EDI can reduce per purchase order cost from between $40 and $150 to $11.20.

At the state level, there has been some effort to automate eligibility, claims, and payment through the use of EDI. In Arkansas, for example, EDI use has increased to more than 80 percent of Medicaid providers. The Automated Eligibility Verification and Claims Submission program conducts on-line eligibility transactions in 20 seconds and pays electronic claims in 7 to 10 days. Reduced claims-processing expenses through 1996 are expected to save the state $1.8 million. For participating providers, electronic claims submission results in a higher percentage of claims being paid upon first submission (in the 1994 fiscal year, 96 percent of electronic claims were paid the first time, compared to 67 percent of paper claims).[14]

Private practices also are discovering the benefits of EDI. In Cleveland, an inner-city practice led by Dr. Harold W. Ford submits claims for Medicaid patients electronically. Payment on claims is normally received within 10 days, at a cost per claim of only 28 cents. Not only does the electronic system require fewer support staff than manual billing, the 10-day turnaround on claims represents a predictable cash flow for the clinic, allowing it to remain solvent while still treating a large indigent population.[15]

Facilities introducing EDI in their business operations have reported numerous cost and quality benefits. River Oaks Hospital, in Jackson, Mississippi, has seen revenues double from increased claims volume, while adding only two FTEs to their business office. Southside Hospital, in Bay Shore, New York, cut bill preparation time to four days or fewer (compared to 10 before automation), also reducing accounts receivable (A/R) from as high as 90 days to as low as 47 days. St. Mary's Hospital, in Richmond, Virginia, combined imaging and EDI technologies, and was able to cut 9 to 11 days out of receivables collection and reduce staff by 15 percent. Staff cut from preparing claims were reassigned to follow up on outstanding ones, reducing A/R from 90 days to fewer than 60.[16]

An emerging area of EDI use, physician office/pharmacy, has shown promise in early studies. In Louisville, a pilot program allows physician offices to route prescriptions to area pharmacies electronically. Participants in the program report time savings for both physician and pharmacy staff; electronic messaging allows pharmacists to query prescriptions, reducing telephone wait time for both offices. Patients receive their prescriptions faster because the electronic system ensures that the prescription order arrives before the patient. Additionally, prescriptions are more legible, eliminating the need to decipher physician handwriting.[17] Another automated system, developed by a company in Fort Lauderdale, Florida, collects drug interaction and managed care company formulary information. In physician offices using the system, formulary compliance rates have jumped to 90 percent, compared to typical compliance rates of 45–60 percent.[18]

Investment Considerations

Although the potential savings through adoption of EDI technologies are large, there are a number of associated costs and concerns that provider organizations must address. Topping the list of EDI considerations is price: Although it has enormous cost-saving potential, EDI is not inexpensive. Fully

58 percent of organizations reporting to WEDI reported cost as the number one barrier to adopting EDI technology.

Telecommunications costs may include use of a value-added network (VAN). In exchange for setup and ongoing maintenance fees, a VAN allows provider organizations to connect through EDI with multiple payers, without maintaining direct EDI links with each. However, VANs are only cost-effective to a point; typically, as the number of transactions increase, so do the fees.

Another cost associated with EDI is maintenance related. To ensure compliance with EDI and contracting agreements, organizations must monitor EDI transactions for volume and data accuracy. Random, periodic evaluation of contract term compliance by trading partners and insurance carriers should be carried out to ensure that contracts, pricing, and data standards are being fully met. Initial agreements must establish some kind of reconciliation policy to resolve disputes, should they occur.

Another particularly troubling issue hindering the widespread adoption of EDI is the lack of health care standardization. In industries such as transportation and wholesale pharmaceuticals, EDI is largely standardized; however, in health care, although many organizations use either HCFA or American National Standards Institute (ANSI) X12 standard data sets for claims submission, various small differences have developed in the application of those data sets. In addition, WEDI estimates that 42 percent of states have either no uniform standard or a customized state standard. For the provider organization, this may mean a completely separate EDI interface for each individual payer.

Continued Growth

Cost pressures will continue to force the adoption of EDI technologies. Already widely accepted at the acute care, inpatient facility level, EDI will soon become a de facto standard for claims submission all the way to the physician office level, as payers react to the economic advantages of electronic submission. Today, significant room for EDI expansion still exists in the physician practice arena. WEDI's 1993 report claims in that year only 12 percent of physician claims were submitted electronically, compared to 70 percent of all hospital claims.[19]

Information Systems Technology

The use of some kind of health care–specific application software is nearly universal at all types of health care facilities. As IS development has progressed from primarily financial and administrative-based applications toward advanced clinical functionalities, logical groupings of systems such as critical clusters have evolved. (See chapter 1.) Table 2-5 reviews the most common IS clusters, as well as the functions typically found within each grouping.

Table 2-5.   Health Care–Specific Application Software and Functionalities

General Financial Systems	Patient Financial and Administrative Systems	Decision Support Systems	Managed Care Systems	Clinical Systems	Ancillary Department Systems	Physician Office Systems	Home Health Systems
• General ledger • Accounts payable • Budget • Fixed assets • Payroll • Human resources • Materials management • Electronic commerce	• Admission/ discharge/ transfer • Registration • Medical records • Scheduling • Patient billing (accounts receivable) • Quality assurance • Utilization review	• Case mix • Budgeting • Cost accounting • Market planning and analysis • Contract management (including reimbursement modeling) • Clinical decision support (including clinical process improvement, clinical paths, and protocols) • Reimbursement modeling • Productivity management • Provider profiling	• Contract management (including reimbursement modeling) • Capitation • Referrals • Authorization and eligibility • Utilization review • Case management • Outcomes • Reporting • Claims, reimbursement • Medical economics • Member services (payer functionality) • Premium billing (payer functionality)	• Order entry • Results reporting • Acuity classification • Nursing • Care plans, protocols • Case management • Clinical process improvement • Provider profiling	• Laboratory • Pharmacy • Radiology • Operating room	• Scheduling • Registration • Patient billing (accounts receivable) • Medical records • Managed care • General financials • Utilization review, case management	• Scheduling • Patient billing, accounts receivable • General financials • Human resources • Clinical documentation • Clinical pathways, protocols • Managed care (including contract management) • Materials management

General Financial Systems

One of the first areas to be automated in provider organizations, general financial functions work to support the basic financial transactions required in the day-to-day operation of a health care enterprise. Information systems typically reduce administrative burdens on staff, focusing on cost consciousness or control efforts. The types of systems include general ledger, accounts payable, fixed assets, payroll, human resources, and materials management.

Materials management systems automate the process through which inventory is ordered, tracked, and distributed. These systems can produce clear economic benefits. Through better control over inventory amounts, storage space can be converted to income-producing offices and staff hours required for inventory maintenance can be reduced. Interfaces with patient administrative systems can accurately track all chargeable patient materials, automatically uploading data to be billed. With this capability, previously lost charges can be captured and recovered.

Patient Financial and Administrative Systems

These systems deal with the multitude of practical, nonmedical aspects of treating patients. In U.S. hospital facilities, patient accounting and on-line admitting are nearly universally automated.[20] The benefits of these systems focus on cost and process improvement because the systems allow staff to use resources more efficiently to capture and process patient information and charges. Types of systems in this cluster include admission, discharge, and transfer; registration; medical records; scheduling; patient accounting; accounts receivable; and quality assurance/utilization review (QA/UR).

Using optical storage in the medical records department is increasingly common at provider organizations, and has led to cost and process benefits. These reported benefits have included reduced or eliminated paper folders, reduced retrieval times for medical record requests, and the ability to provide multi-user access to patient data. Memorial Sloan-Kettering Cancer Center, in New York City, began optically capturing and storing enterprisewide receivables data—with a 22-month payback on its investment. Savings came from reduced FTE requirements, media savings (paper, microfiche, microfilm), space savings, and productivity gains of up to 50 percent or more.[21]

Medical records systems increasingly are incorporating advanced functionality designed to improve and streamline the daily work of medical records staffers. A number of current systems have the functional ability to prompt physicians to complete charts while patients are still in the hospital, reducing required follow-up time by departmental staff and increasing billing turnaround time.

When the Methodist Health Group, in Indianapolis, replaced an existing transcription system with one that had newer, more up-to-date functionality, it found that clinical coders made tremendous gains in productivity. Within one month's time, the amount of unbilled (uncoded) accounts was reduced by $800,000. In addition, through combining the automation effort with a reengineering initiative, department staffing was reduced by 25 percent over six months. Medical staff now have on-line access to transcribed reports, giving them the information they need in a more timely fashion and reducing the burden of requests on the medical records department.[22]

Throughout the health care industry, one overwhelmingly overlooked area for automation is the mail room. Hospitals studying this area have been astonished at the volume of resources being spent to investigate, readdress, and resend bills incorrectly addressed. Many hospitals have reported significant cost savings from the installation of automated address stamp and verification systems. These systems automatically check addresses at admission, issuing an alert if the address is undeliverable; change abbreviations to postal standards; and presort, bar-code, and bundle mail to qualify for postal discounts.

Decision Support Systems

As organizations realize the need to collect and analyze data in more complex ways, decision support systems have emerged as one of the leading technologies of the 1990s. Initially, research and development focused on the financial activities that could be supported and improved. Today, clinical decision support, with incorporated quality and outcomes functionalities, is growing rapidly in use and popularity.

The most commonly reported benefit of financial decision support relates to the extensive and versatile data modeling and reporting capabilities of decision support systems. Through use of a system, organizations can pull raw data from various points of care and then relate those data to ongoing trends or services they wish to study. Typical reports include:

- Medicare to total populations
- Physician performance (top admitters, charges by specialty, LOS, case mix)
- Profit by service line
- Admission by service area
- Inpatient versus outpatient populations
- FTE, division comparisons
- Revenue versus expenses

Clinical decision support is a strong support tool for clinical research activities. Intermountain HealthCare (Salt Lake City) uses a clinical information system to collect and analyze data for developing clinical protocols. One such protocol, related to treatment of pressure ulcers, lowered organizational costs and improved patient outcomes. Another protocol, a standardized method for treating adult respiratory distress syndrome (ARDS) in a pulmonary intensive care unit, improved survival rates from 9.5 to 45 percent. Intermountain uses its IS technology to constantly review and revise protocols, as more data are collected.[23]

Decision support technology is fast becoming an important component of broad-scale disease and case management programs. To study a particular condition and formulate the most effective clinical treatment, accurate, specific data on the disease and its manifestations, treatments, and typical outcomes are essential. The (Seattle) Group Health Cooperative of Puget Sound's Clinical Roadmap program uses technology to help physicians better manage patient populations according to their clinical needs.[24]

Managed Care Systems

With their ability to handle multiple and complex contract and capitation arrangements, managed care systems are generating tremendous interest among provider organizations facing the threat or reality of managed care. However, the features and functionalities of managed care and clinical decision support systems sometimes overlap.

The use of contract management systems to manage multiple managed care arrangements has exploded across the industry. Some estimates project a staggering 450 percent growth in contract management purchases (sometimes seen as part of a decision support package) by the end of the decade.[25] The most commonly reported benefits of these systems include an increased ability to accept and execute managed care contracts, recouped revenue from the capability to audit existing contracts, and the ability to handle increased managed care business without increasing FTE staff. Additionally, because complex contract terms are compared automatically against cases, loss limits are adhered to, protecting provider organizations from suffering extraordinary expenses for unusual cases.

On the payer side, technologies are being used to process and adjudicate claims against managed care contract terms. United HealthCare Corporation, a payer operating out of Minnetonka, Minnesota, uses artificial intelligence technology to adjudicate claims, using predefined rules to review and evaluate claims, freeing medical analyst staff to concentrate on extremely complex cases. The system conducts nearly one million reviews each month, eventually referring 3 percent for medical analyst review. Through this technology, United HealthCare has reduced its claims-processing costs from $1.23 (manual processing) to $.15.[26]

Clinical Systems

Clinical systems are those that contribute to the direct management of patient care activities. The experiences of provider organizations with clinical systems have become increasingly available as these systems become more common. Systems in this cluster include order-entry and results reporting, nursing documentation (including care plans, protocols), acuity classification, and case management. Typically reported benefits include improved speed and accuracy in charting, smoother policy and procedural changes, time savings in transfer summaries and drug calculations, and research data-gathering capabilities.

Nursing systems have been widely studied for their impact on nursing work flow as well as the incidence of adverse drug events. Commonly reported benefits include overtime reduction or elimination (for nursing staff), improved nurse recruiting efforts, and reduced medication errors. In New Jersey, the Nursing Incentive Reimbursement Aware (NIRA) project reported mixed financial benefits[27] of nursing systems, although staff did report a number of other benefits from system use, including improved nursing care through diagnostic prompts, forced timely documentation of care, some time savings for nursing staff, and improved patient satisfaction, because nurses spent more time in patient rooms.

After Concord Hospital, in central New Hampshire, implemented a bedside terminal system, the impact of the system on nurse care time, RN overtime, and unit medication error rates was studied. Postimplementation, the hospital found that though nursing overtime decreased by 42 percent, medication error rates remained stable and nursing time in direct care activities actually decreased by 7 percent. However, study designers could not attribute this decrease directly to use of the system, suggesting that other organizational factors (such as staff reduction and work redesign efforts) may have contributed.[28]

Persuading clinicians to use IS technology has been a subject of much interest in the health care industry. For example, a number of organizations have found the benefits of direct physician order entry to be compelling. At LDS Hospital, in Salt Lake City, the automated system allows physicians to compare a patient's medical history against drug information prior to writing a prescription. LDS, whose internal estimates judge that each medication error costs $2,000 to treat, believes it now is avoiding a million dollars in treatment costs annually through use of automation. The system alerts physicians to known patient allergies and monitors clinical indicators after medication is administered for possible adverse reactions. Since installing the system, LDS's medication error rate has gone from 6 adverse drug events (ADEs) per 100 admissions to 2.7 ADEs per 100 admissions.[29]

When William N. Wishard Memorial Hospital (Indianapolis) provided automated medical records access to a medical-surgical unit, drug-related incidents dropped by one-third, saving $900 per patient. The system automatically blocks clinicians from ordering more than the daily dose of a medication for a patient, checks for past allergic reactions, and makes educational information available for on-line review.[30]

In Boston, Brigham and Women's Hospital (B&W) uses an automated order-entry system to manage costs and maintain clinical quality. The system currently identifies 320 of some 4,000 daily medication orders as possible duplicates, allowing clinicians to cancel the order before unnecessary costs are incurred. Another 29 orders are flagged as potentially interacting with existing medications. Through use of automation, the hospital estimates that it saves $1.5 million annually in adverse drug reaction costs and an additional $100,000 in eliminated redundant tests. Although using the system means physicians spend an extra 20 to 30 minutes entering orders each day, the hospital has found the potential benefits so compelling that staff are required to use the system. Total ROI for the system from 1993 to 1995, says B&W, reached 326 percent.[31]

At Jacobi Medical Center in New York City, the transition to automated medical records technology has begun. However, even in the early stages of implementation, the hospital has seen a 16 percent drop in duplicated inpatient test orders—the automated order-entry system alerts staff when a test has already been administered. Physicians at Jacobi like the order-entry capabilities, 76 percent of them reporting in a 1994 survey that they felt it made them more efficient.[32]

More than one insurance company is offering malpractice premium discounts to physicians who install and use software applications with quality and risk control functionalities. Such functionalities—reminders of tests, interaction alerts, alerts of variance from prescribed treatments, diagnostic and treatment prompts—not only help ensure the quality of care but also offer cost-control and documentation benefits to physicians.[33]

Ancillary Department Systems

Ancillary systems manage activities internal to individual hospital departments. The departments most commonly characterized in this fashion are pharmacy, radiology, and laboratory, although others, such as physical therapy or the operating room (OR), may be included. Typically, these systems provide better work flow tracking and analysis, affording staff gains in productivity or education.

Pharmacy benefits frequently are associated with the networking capabilities inherent in order-entry systems. With orders electronically transmitted from the point of care, pharmacy staff can fill prescriptions in a more timely manner, reducing patient wait time and increasing patient satisfaction. The automatic inventory of medications enables optimum use of both cash and medication storage space, reducing the sheer volume of controlled substances that must be tracked and maintained.

At the University of Wisconsin Hospitals and Clinics, in Madison, a robotic drug distribution system is used to fill 90 percent of prescription orders. Since its implementation, the error rate of prepared prescriptions has been .02 percent, compared to a 1.43 percent error rate from manual orders. The system paid for itself in 2.3 years.[34]

Automated medication systems, often posted at points of care within the hospital, provide economic and quality benefits. One nine-month study of medication administration at a Dallas teaching hospital correlated use of an automated medication dispensing system with a reduction in medication errors. At the study hospital, the error rate dropped from 16.9 to 10.4 percent.[35]

The University of California at San Francisco (UCSF) Medical Center also implemented an automated drug distribution system. After implementation, the number of missing doses dropped significantly. Through time-and-motion studies, UCSF examined the work load of pharmacy and nursing staff. Postautomation, the amount of pharmacist time spent on routine functions decreased; nursing staff also benefited from time savings associated with the system.[36]

Radiology systems, particularly as imaging technologies continue to improve, can offer numerous benefits to provider organizations. To aid in controlling the long-term costs of chronic lung disease (including chronic tuberculosis), the National Jewish Center for Immunology and Respiratory Medicine in Denver plans to link national laboratories with regional tuberculosis centers, eventually adding the National Institutes of Health (NIH) and the Centers for Disease Control (CDC). Through this project, called TeleMed, providers will have access to a repository of radiographic images and clinical information. Diagnosed early, multiple drug–resistant TB costs nearly $10,000 to treat, whereas in later stages the cost can skyrocket to $200,000–$250,000 per patient.[37]

Laboratory systems, such as those in pharmacy and radiology, offer potential benefits beyond the bounds of the department. After implementing a laboratory information system, Phoenixville Hospital in Pennsylvania found that clinical staff made fewer telephone calls to the lab. The system allows clinicians to view test results on-line from nursing stations, the physician lounge, and other places, rather than requiring a call to the lab.[38] Washington Hospital Center, in Washington, DC, implemented a point-of-care laboratory technology that uses single-use cartridges and biosensors to deliver panels of up to eight test results right to the patient's bedside. Using this system, clinicians can have test results directly at the point of care in less than two minutes. Fully integrated with the hospital's main laboratory information system (LIS), the point-of-care device automatically downloads results into the LIS, saving further time and reducing the possibility of clerical transcription error. Using the system brought Washington Hospital an added benefit, because the very small blood sample required by the system helped reduce anemia among neonatal intensive care unit (NICU) patients.[39]

Continued Growth

As health care organizations continue to grow and consolidate across the continuum of care, application system technologies that offer benefits to a wide audience of users will continue to gain prominence. As managed care makes further inroads into care delivery, more and advanced functionalities will be developed and delivered. Historically less-automated markets, such as home health care physician practice, will continue moving toward computerizing many of their activities.

Benefit Values

Not every organization will achieve high benefit levels through the use of automation. Management, organizational, and technological factors may conspire to delay or prevent positive returns. However, all the organizations discussed here made the effort to clearly plan for the returns of technology, incrementally increasing its inherent worth. To achieve breakthrough returns, provider organizations must adopt a consistent program of pushing technologies for added value and must integrate IT with redesign initiatives. Studying the achievement of other organizations can help extend the boundaries of ROI, making new or previously unconsidered benefits possible.

References

1. Simpson, R. L., and Nauright, L. P. Benefits of hospital information systems as seen by front-line staff. *Proceedings of the 1994 Annual HIMSS Conference* 4:381–90.

2. Dunbar, C. MultiCare Health System saves millions of dollars through redesigned care. *Health Management Technology* 15(8):22–29, July 1994.

3. Dunbar, C. Allina Health tackles seven I/S projects in new merger. *Health Management Technology* 15(13):22, Dec. 1994.

4. Sundeen, M., and Lohman, P. Reader survey asks who controls costs with I/S. *Health Management Technology* 15(7):30–33, June 1994.

5. Young, J. K. Contrasting approaches aim at similar network goals. *Computers in Healthcare* 14(3):43–45, Mar. 1993.

6. Barnard, D. C. Effect of advances in technology on telephone service strategy. *Proceedings of the 1994 Annual HIMSS Conference* 2:349–59.

7. Odell, D. Wireless phones give nurses more time with patients. *Healthcare Informatics* 12(10):78–79, Oct. 1995.

8. Low-cost predictive dialer boosts hospitals' cash flow. *National Report on Computers and Health* 15(14):2–3, July 4, 1994.

9. Whitney, C., and Keers, S. Telecommunications and TQM: managing technology to improve customer satisfaction. *Proceedings of the 1994 Annual HIMSS Conference* 3:213–25.

10. Siwicki, B. Starting engine saves money. *Health Data Management* 3(8):26–27, Sept. 1995.

11. Computer-Based Patient Record Privacy Survey, conducted by Gordon and Glickson, Chicago, copyright 1995.

12. Internet adolescence. *The Network Strategy Report* 8(10), Sept. 1994.

13. Workgroup on Electronic Data Interchange (WEDI). *The 1993 WEDI Report,* Oct. 1993. The full description and methodology of the study (conducted by the Tiber Group) is available in section 7, pages 25–36.

14. Medicaid program removes the hassle. *Health Data Management* 2(5):36–38, June 1994.

15. Steenhuysen, J. Automation keeps inner-city practice afloat. *Health Data Management* 2(5):21–25, June 1994.

16. Watson, S. How automation is breaking the cash flow logjam. *Health Data Management* 2(5):53–60, June 1994.

17. Siwicki, B. Electronic prescriptions: just what the doctor ordered. *Health Data Management* 3(10):62–68, Nov. 1995.

18. Siwicki.

19. Workgroup on Electronic Data Interchange (WEDI).

20. Society for Healthcare Planning and Marketing. *Working Together to Shape the Future: Environmental Assessment 93/94.* Chicago: American Hospital Association, 1993.

21. McBride, J. S., and Schwegman, P. M. Enterprise integration of document imaging. *Proceedings of the 1994 Annual HIMSS Health Care Conference and Exhibition* 3:67–79.

22. Wear, P. K., French, W. R., and Petrosky, C. Physicians and electronic signature authentication. Proceedings of the Toward an Electronic Patient Record '96 Conference, San Diego, CA, May 13–18, 1996, 1:209–15.

23. Getting a head start on applying automation. *Health Data Management* 2(5):28–29, June 1994.

24. Bazzoli, F. Information technology essential to HMO's disease management strategy. *Health Data Management* 4(1):31, Jan. 1996.

25. Morrisey, J. Providers get their due. *Modern Healthcare* 24(15):60–66, Nov. 7, 1994.

26. Knowles, A. United HealthCare: a bargain at 15 cents. *CIO* 9(8):42–44, Feb. 1, 1996.

27. Hendrickson, G., Kovner, C. T., Knickman, J. R., and Finkler, S. A. Implementation of a variety of computerized bedside nursing information systems in 17 New Jersey hospitals. *Computers in Nursing* 13(3):96–102, May–June 1995.

28. Brown, S. J., Cioffi, M. A., Schinella, P., and Shaw, A. Evaluation of the impact of a bedside terminal system in a rapidly changing community hospital. *Computers in Nursing* 13(6):280–84, Nov.–Dec. 1995.

29. Bazzoli, F. Medication errors: automation holds promise of prevention. *Health Data Management* 3(8):30–39, Sept. 1995.

30. Bazzoli.

31. Fabris, P. Brigham and Women's Hospital: a speedy recovery. *CIO* 9(8):34–36, Feb. 1, 1996.

32. Bazzoli, F. Preparing for a managed care shift. *Health Data Management* 3(7):42–43, July–Aug. 1995.

33. Malpractice insurers offer discounts for doctors using electronic records. *Health Data Management* 3(2):14, Feb. 1995.

34. Bazzoli, Medication errors.

35. Borel, J., and Rascati, K. L. Effect of an automated, nursing-unit-based drug-dispensing device on medication errors. *American Journal of Health System Pharmacy* 52:1875–79, Sept. 1, 1995.

36. Schwarz, H. O., and Brodowy, B. A. Implementation and evaluation of an automated dispensing system. *American Journal of Health System Pharmacy* 52:823–28, Apr. 15, 1995.

37. Los Alamos rolls out technology transfer project for radiology. *Health Management Technology* 15(12):42–46, Nov. 1994.

38. Ericson, K., and Farrell, C. Serving clients in the lab. *Healthcare Informatics* 12(8):72–78 Aug. 1995.

39. Winner, P., and Chappie, A. Streamlining lab services: point-of-care technology. *Healthcare Informatics* 12(8):68–70, Aug. 1995.

Emerging Technologies and Their Impact

Many health care information technologies (ITs) currently in use were at one point considered risky investments by provider organizations. Equipment such as the personal computer (PC) and functionalities such as automatic bill generation, electronic claims submission, and appointment scheduling, once considered cutting edge, now are essential requirements for provider organizations. They have fundamentally changed the nature and requirements of work in the industry, becoming a necessary and accepted part of conducting business. Today, further advances in technology have the potential to effect similar fundamental change.

Core IT development tool sets, allowing increased flexibility and cost efficiency in the custom development of technology solutions, continue to expand and evolve. The progression toward visual, intuitive (GUI) computing has expanded users, and technical interoperability and interface capabilities have reduced the scope and financial requirements for start-up development. The environment for new and emerging technologies is more fertile than ever before.

For provider organizations, this rapidly advancing technology offers tremendous potential for benefits return. Indeed, for a provider organization to achieve breakthrough, transforming benefit levels, the organization most likely will have to invest in emerging technologies. This chapter deals specifically with the potentials and pitfalls of these new health care technologies. Discussion focuses on the different strategies and approaches required to successfully implement and utilize emerging technologies, as well as the breakthrough benefits potential associated with such projects. Specific discussion topics include:

- How and why emerging technology strategy differs from mainstream information system (IS) decision making
- Assessing, acquiring, or developing emerging technology—how to select from the alternatives
- When costs outweigh benefits—making the decision to walk away from invested money

Finally, the chapter surveys today's emerging technology groups. These groups—application software, advanced networking and communications, and clinical process technologies—all offer widespread potential in health care through enhanced support for the storage, analysis, presentation, and dissemination of information, locally or remotely. These capabilities, not yet fully proven from either a cost or technology perspective, offer potential support for cost-effective, quality-enhancing changes in the delivery and management of health care.

Defining Emerging Technology

For the purposes of this discussion, an *emerging technology* is one that meets one or more of the following criteria:

- The systems are not yet available via general public release, installed only at experimental or beta-site organizations.
- The systems have been on the market less than three years, in any industry.
- There are a limited number of "live" health care installations using the technology.
- In health care, the technology has been in use for less than two years (even if it has been widely used in other sectors such as banking, airlines, and retail sales for a longer period). The technology's adaptability and transferability to the health care environment are not yet proven.
- There is a lack of a dominant standard in the marketplace for the technology.

Currently, some of the most visible and well-publicized health care information technologies, such as electronic medical records (EMRs) and patient interactive systems, meet these criteria. When dealing with technology of this nature, provider organizations face a level of risk not seen in more routine IT purchases. At the same time, the potential rewards from the use of such emerging technology can bring an organization breakthrough economic and strategic gains. Over the long term, such gains may only be possible through the early use of unproven technology, developed within the context of a relationship with a technology supplier or through self-development or customization.

A technology can be said to have "emerged" when one or more of the following criteria are met:

- In the case of packaged application software, the technology is commercially available with multiple (20 or more) installation sites; is based on multiple, progressive versions; and has been on the market to health care providers for three or more years.

- The technology, particularly application technology such as electronic data interchange (EDI), is in use in some form at more than 25 percent of major health care provider sites.
- There are prevailing technical and implementation standards for the technology, such as the current American National Standards Institute (ANSI) banking EDI or Institute of Electrical and Electronics Engineers (IEEE) Ethernet network standards.

Commercial Viability

In health care, provider organizations continue to struggle with the rapidly evolving information requirements of vertical and horizontal service delivery integration, managed care, population-based medicine, and health care reform. It is extremely common for a gap to exist between the emergence of an IT need and the full development of the application technology to meet that need. Before a technology becomes commercially viable, developers and investors must accept an increased level of risk in their efforts. Technology suppliers judge the commercial viability of developing related application systems in a number of ways, including:

- The potential marketplace must be large enough to spread the investment cost over the anticipated number of unit sales.
- The investment cost must be reasonable and affordable.
- Application or technology development must be technically feasible, supported by other available low-risk technologies.
- An organization must exist that is willing to serve as a development site and a reference customer.

Until such time as these indicators exist, technology and software suppliers working in the area are hesitant to commit to large investment efforts. Provider organizations that are early adopters of these technologies consequently face larger financial and technical risks. At the same time, by accepting this risk, these organizations have the potential to achieve larger benefit returns.

Technologies Supporting an Emerging Technology Program

Over the course of the past decade, technology suppliers have put tremendous effort into reconciling internal programming and technical requirements with the need to produce commercially appealing application systems. Toward that end, suppliers have developed and enhanced a number of critical support technologies, dealing with both the front-end user to computer interface and back-end technical or architectural requirements. The success of these technologies has fundamentally shifted the market for developing application software and technology, easing financial and risk barriers, enlarging potential economic returns, shortening application development timetables, and thereby creating opportunities for new companies and products. Figure 3-1 illustrates some of the tool set technologies available today.

Database tools, including relational database technology, provide a mechanism for large-scale, flexible data storage and retrieval. The ability to store large data sets is increasingly important in health care as providers continue to integrate care across the continuum.

Correspondingly, *data access and manipulation tools* ease rigid data storage requirements by providing relatively storage-independent mechanisms for requesting and analyzing unique data subsets. Preprogrammed reporting, with ad hoc capabilities, is a universal functionality; structured query languages and query by example capabilities allow users to request and obtain precisely the data in which they are interested.

Interface engines have emerged over the past several years as one of the most important enabling development technologies. They provide logical connectivity between incompatible hardware platforms, translating data messages sent from different applications in different formats. Through investment in this technology, provider organizations are able to avoid significant hardware or software reinvestment costs as they plan and implement enterprisewide networks and application systems. (Interface engine technology is discussed in more detail later in this chapter.)

User interface tools affect the way data are presented to technology end users and the way end users access the technology. Graphical user interfaces, with "point-and-click" technology, continue to be heavily developed for their intuitive appeal. Other user access technologies currently enjoying heavy development include light wand, pen-based, and voice activation systems.

Figure 3-1. Application Technology Development Tool Sets

Data Access and Manipulation Tools	User Interface Tools
Storage-independent mechanisms for data analysis • Reporting tools (preformatted, SQL, FOCUS, ad hoc) • Interface engines	End-user access and presentation • Graphical user interface • Data visualization • Light pen, voice • 3D, multimedia tools
Database Tools	**Development Environment Tools**
Provide rapid, flexible data access • Relational database technologies (Sybase, Informix, Oracle, RDB, DB2, Ingres)	Used to build new technology features/ functionalities Enablers: Object-oriented, open systems, client/server • Application development tools (PowerBuilder, Gupta, NeXT, Smalltalk)

In the data and network security arena, experimentation continues with biosecurity tools, including fingerprint and retinal scanning devices. More advanced data visualization work, using three-dimensional and multimedia technology, promise further ease in the use of developing applications.

Development environment tools provide technology developers a powerful and flexible mechanism on which to build their new technology. With the onset of object-oriented programming, a more flexible, less-resource-intensive methodology for writing application software, programmers can more easily incorporate sophisticated capabilities into their programs. Open systems technology, allowing interoperability between hardware and software components regardless of the originating developer/supplier, further eases the financial and technical requirements for application development. For technology end users, the growth of client/server technology allows smaller-scaled investments with well-controlled system growth and advanced development technologies and applications. No longer does the end user have to replace entire systems; with client/server technology, small-scale, prioritized investments are feasible.

Together, these critical support technologies have contributed to successive generations of information systems that are faster and more visually attractive, are easier to use and maintain, and offer more sophisticated functionality than systems and technologies of the past.

Developing an Emerging Technology Program

In working with emerging technologies, provider organizations must grapple with the lack of existing data on the technology's technical and strategic capabilities. This sometimes considerable inherent difficulty can be partially compensated for by a structured, methodical approach—both strategic and operational—to selecting and managing emerging technologies, and integrating them into the enterprise IT strategy.

Provider Strategy and Operations: The Emerging Technology Oversight Group

The effective use of emerging technology requires a long-term commitment to achieving and maintaining success. The rapid and evolving nature of an emerging technology requires constant oversight from an overall technology perspective as well as by specific initiative. A steering committee or management council, with members offering diverse financial, strategic, operational, technical, and end-user backgrounds, can effectively direct an emerging technology program supporting business and medical organizational goals.

Key to establishing and maintaining such a group is developing a cross-disciplinary approach to emerging technology investment. The group's clear focus should be on establishing and evaluating technologies by using a return on investment (ROI) methodology designed to maximize returns and judge acceptable levels of organizational risk. Appendix B illustrates a sample charter for such a group (called here the Emerging Technology Oversight Group, or ETOG).

There are other important characteristics that help to ensure a successful emerging technology investment. Some of these include:

- The existence of formulated guidelines, strategies, policies, and funding caps for experimenting with, acquiring, and managing emerging technologies.
- The use of a consistent, established methodology for assessing new technologies—one that considers the requirements of multiple disciplines.
- The leadership of technology executives with strong project management skills.
- The adoption of a "go slow, prove it" approach: staged investments, prototypes, pilots, proven benefits, continuous feedback cycles.
- A willingness on the part of management to walk away from a project that is not providing value to the organization, learn from the experience, and move on.

This final characteristic—a willingness on the part of the organization to fail—often is the most difficult for an organization to accept. However, it is one of the most important success characteristics when dealing with risky and unproven technologies.

The use of committee oversight in managing emerging technologies can provide organizations with clear and balanced project guidance and direction. Often such committees are formed because of a specific project. Typically, they are tasked with reviewing and evaluating technologies, considering project management alternatives, selecting and overseeing a project team, and setting and monitoring benefit expectations and budgets. Whether by committee or other oversight mechanism, once an organization makes a commitment to acquire and use emerging technologies, the risk and reward spectrum is determined by the chosen development and project management approach.

Emerging Technology Development Options

Emerging technology projects, by their nature, typically require some level of custom software development (as opposed to packaged software purchase), though not necessarily by the provider organization itself. Three scenarios—alpha custom development by the organization, alpha development site for technology supplier, and supplier/provider partnership—are available for providers interested in the use and benefits of emerging technology. Each alternative offers a somewhat different level of risk and reward to the provider organization.

In some cases, health care organizations conceive, develop, and implement an emerging technology on their own — a process sometimes referred to as *alpha custom development*. As the originator and ongoing sponsor of the technology, the provider fully controls its scope and functionalities, and any ultimate commercial rewards from the product accrue to the organization. At the same time, as the developer, the provider carries the full burden of financial, technical, and achievement risk.

Organizations selecting this approach typically share a number of characteristics, including relative financial security, strong information technology competencies (particularly in project management), capable users, and a strong "user champion" (a user who understands the potential and benefits of technology and actively lobbies to support IT initiatives).

Other organizations, desiring to minimize the sometimes heavy financial and technological risks of custom development, may choose to become an *alpha development site* for a technology supplier. In this situation, the provider organization acts as a test site, allowing the supplier the opportunity to test and adjust the functionalities of its new information systems. In a smaller-scale variant to this approach, some providers choose to act as a product beta site, performing the same functions for new versions of products already in general release.

These organizations frequently are similar to organizations choosing to develop systems themselves, but are unable or unwilling to accept the full burden of development risk. They may not be financially secure, or they may not have a strong enough competency in IT to drive a full-scale development effort.

Finally, some organizations prefer a more collaborative effort, a *supplier/ provider partnership,* where all participants share the risks and rewards of the development initiative. Assuming the technology eventually becomes marketable, participants may share user license and royalty fees. Full ownership of the technology most commonly resides with the technology supplier.

Emerging Technology Assessment

When considering an emerging technology investment, providers should first and always consider the fundamental motivation for the investment (for example, what advantage will it bring the organization). Motivations may include strategic need, immediate or short-term problem solving, economic gains, or positioning for benefits — incremental or breakthrough — at some later point. Whatever the reason, the goals behind the investment should be clear and agreeable to the primary constituents (board, steering committee, user groups) involved.

Investments motivated by a desire for breakthrough economics almost always involve a longer payback period, perhaps three to seven years. Payback comes in a combination of quantified gains and more difficult to measure improvements in the competitive position of the organization. The EMR long-range plan presented in chapter 4 shows overall negative financial returns to the provider organization for the first five years of development. From year three onward, however, economic returns begin to multiply exponentially.

In contrast, incremental investments typically adopt a much shorter frame of return. Implementation cycles may be only three to twelve months, and the payback period may be no more than two years — preferably one or less. Chapter 2 discusses a number of organizations that recouped initial technology investments rapidly and decisively.

The specific considerations behind an investment in emerging technology will differ according to the organization's goals and objectives, as well as underlying investment motivations. Providers considering such an investment should review the potential project from technology, organization, and local market viewpoints. Table 3-1 offers a side-by-side comparison of the primary areas to evaluate in the investment decision-making process.

Table 3-1. Evaluating an Emerging Technology Investment

Investment Motivation to Support Need	The Emerging Technology	The Health Care Organization and Local Market
Breakthrough	• Duration and extent of market "proof" of the technology • Vendor resources to support the technology over the long term	• Projected information requirements of external organizations • Advantages derived by competitors from use of the emerging technology • Extent to which the technology aligns with and supports the medium- and long-range business goals of the organization • Financial pressure on investments to provide immediate returns
Incremental	• Short-term availability of technology on the market • Short implementation cycle; vendor support for accelerated implementation • Immediate benefits from use of the emerging technology	• Urgency of investment due to successful, competitive use of technology by competitor • Financial and human resources available to support rapid implementation of the technology

The Technology

In examining emerging technologies, provider organizations should not only examine the technology itself, but also the suppliers developing the technology. Important issues to consider include the length of time the technology has been available (in health care or other markets) and the extent of current use by provider organizations. When evaluating suppliers, providers should evaluate how well positioned the vendor is in the market and how committed it is to remaining in health care. Also important to examine is the vendor's strategic orientation toward the future of the technology and the financial resources available toward further product research and development.

Emerging technology can provide incremental benefits to providers either by addressing existing process problems or through meeting unusual short-term needs. The true potential of emerging technology, however, is clearly for breakthrough positioning and benefits realization. In planning a breakthrough approach, provider organizations must clearly consider the investment risk factors involved.

One risk lies in the depth of the vendor/developer's commitment to the technology over time. The clearest indications of this commitment include available financial and staff resources — for the entire company as well as for those dedicated to the product itself. The percentage of revenues the vendor spends annually on research and development efforts is an additional indicator of its dedication to future development and progress.

The vendor's planned time schedule for developing the emerging technology, and the provider organization's assessment of its feasibility, can help providers forecast the technology's ROI cycle and identify the volume and rate of benefits achievement. Provider organizations should then compare those benefit projections, the technology's cost, and current and projected functionality against their own business plan to validate and support the business case for investing.

The Organization and Local Market

For provider organizations considering the added risks of an emerging technology, a clear and candid evaluation of internal and external factors, such as available financing, internal staff capabilities, local market, and competitive environments, can clearly forecast the likelihood of the technology's success.

Provider organizations in this situation should always consider the framework within which that technology is and will be used. A close look at other local market organizations will indicate both how well received the technology is in the local market as well as the strategic intentions of the competition. For example, a competitor using telemedicine to allow remote consultations may be positioning to achieve a number of benefits, including cost efficiencies in servicing remote market areas, increased market share, and extension of existing specialty service lines or centers of excellence (for example, cardiology, orthopedics). Given this information, other provider groups may choose to initiate or accelerate their own plans for telemedicine, or simply keep a watchful eye on the project results.

Another part of the provider evaluation should focus on reform and regulation. Ongoing changes at federal, state, and local levels can affect the use and usefulness of an emerging technology. In addition, new and changing requirements from external agencies such as the Joint Commission on Accreditation of Healthcare Organizations, the National Committee for Quality Assurance, and various payers and industry purchasing groups and business coalitions can significantly affect the development cycle of an emerging technology.

Organization and market incremental benefits center around meeting changing market and business requirements (such as regulatory changes or new payer-driven reporting requirements). The breakthrough potentials are more strategic in nature, relating to mid- to long-term IS plans and goals. Early adoption of emerging technologies, done well, can give provider organizations critical competitive advantage; it is important for organizations to remain aware of the projects under way or in planning stages throughout their local market.

The Risks of Emerging Technologies

Implementing a new information system or technology always involves risk for the user organization. However, the unique characteristics of emerging technologies can leave provider organizations particularly vulnerable to certain types of risk, relating to selection and use of the technology as well as the supplier supporting it.

Risk Assessment

The primary types of risk surrounding emerging technologies, typically associated with breakthrough benefit potential, include technical risk, vendor risk, and implementation and usage risk.

Technical risk may involve failure of a technology to prove commercially viable after beta testing. This may occur because either a new technology is unsound or the vendor does not have the resources to address problems within the development cycle required by the organization. It also may occur due to outright technology failure (for example, distributed databases do not support EMR response time requirements).

Technical risk also may occur when a technology developer adopts a standard early on that ultimately is not accepted by the market. This poses a problem if the technology was adopted with a view toward long-term usage and payback; the problem is less serious if the technology was acquired in order to resolve an immediate problem and the system has a short payback period. Failure of a new technology to become standard can be due to inadequate marketing clout supporting the technology; industry standards are not always determined by the technical superiority of the contending options.

Vendor risks lie primarily with the possibility of business failure, acquisition, or financial reverse. Any of these circumstances may impair or destroy vendor support for product development, implementation, and problem resolution. Risks are considerably greater for start-up, single-product firms than for well-established ones with diversified lines of market-proven products.

In some situations, technology suppliers choose to abandon a particular technology. This may occur as a result of vendor financial concerns or due to acquisition of the vendor by an outside firm. The risk of this occurrence is significant; high development and marketing costs are driving the health care IS industry through a period of rapid consolidation.

Implementation and usage risks may arise from a number of situations: if the organization is unprepared to accept new ways of accomplishing tasks, if users and operators are inadequately trained, if users perceive the technology as a way to eliminate their jobs, or if the system fails to perform as specified. These risks, which exist for all new system implementation projects, are particularly intense for new technologies. Such technologies often require significant changes in the way people work with each other and in the way they obtain and use data.

Risk Management

Risk management strategies exist to minimize all of these potential problems, and should be vigorously pursued at all phases of the systems life cycle. The more unproven a technology is, the more effort and planning that must be devoted to all phases of the systems life cycle:

- System planning
- Vendor selection and contracting
- System implementation
- System maintenance, usage, and development

System Planning

Taking steps to avoid all potential risks (technical, vendor, implementation, and usage) is critical during the system planning phase. Usually, the system planning process involves a tactical plan (covering the one- to three-year period within the strategic design) and a strategic design (covering the four- to seven-year period). The tactical plan generally focuses on achieving the incremental benefits available from emerging technologies and laying the foundation for any future breakthrough gains. The strategic component concentrates on breakthrough, large-scale benefits realization. In addition to these parts of the plan, the organization should define a 10-year strategic vision for its business and information systems. For each planning horizon, organizations should assess the appropriateness of investing in emerging technologies.

The ETOG should seek information on new technologies and applications. This strategy could include reviewing literature (inside and outside health care), attending national conferences, visiting sites that are testing or using emerging technologies, and visiting vendor research and development groups. Then, information should be disseminated within the organization.

Next, the scope and timing of specific expected benefits should be defined. If strategic benefits are of paramount importance, it may be reasonable to acquire a system that is in beta test but will, if successful, provide breakthrough returns for the organization over the next 5 to 10 years. If incremental considerations are more important, or solutions are required for immediate problems, it may be wiser to select technologies that are commercially available and proven in other industries, with a record of rapid payback.

Potential technologies should then be measured against the standards and guidelines set by the ETOG. Is the investment likely to return an acceptable level of value to the organization? Does the functionality of the technology support current and/or anticipated business or medical goals of the organization?

At this point, the organization's readiness to adopt the new technology should be assessed. The following questions can be used as a starting point for this evaluation:

- How does the proposed technology fit the organization's business plan and IS plan? Is the organization seeking incremental change or a breakthrough? Is the organization committed to keeping legacy or in-place systems, or can the system be redesigned from the ground up?
- Is there a clear management commitment to, and mandate for, the systems change?
- Are financial resources adequate to go through the entire systems life cycle?
- What cost justification is required for the proposed investment?
- Have physicians and other clinical caregivers had their needs and concerns adequately addressed?
- Are users and managers resistant to change or do they welcome it? (This applies to acceptance of change in general, and to change of the specific type that would occur with implementation of a new system.)
- Do the required skills to use, implement, and exploit the technology exist in the IS department and in the user departments?

Finally, the project team, the ETOG, and senior organizational management should lay the groundwork for change. At this point, the expected strategic and tactical benefits, as well as any potential risks, of adopting the technology should have been defined. These risks and rewards should be clearly communicated to constituents (such as the board, senior management, physicians, and staff).

Realistically, the success of any emerging technology project requires the involvement and acceptance of this constituent community. Many organizations have found it helpful to involve key groups — such as physicians and nurses, other critical managers/users — directly in upfront planning activities. Whatever their level of involvement, all organizations (and groups within organizations) potentially affected by a system should be given a voice in the planning and implementation process. Some technologies, such as clinical data repositories (CDRs), potentially affect multiple departments or divisions. The ability to access a list of current patient medications, for example, would affect the work procedures of clinic staff, hospital nursing staff, and home health workers, among others.

The new system should be positioned as a way to improve quality of care and to streamline the tedious, frustrating parts of staff jobs. It is uncommon for new system implementations to allow major reductions in head count; it is important that unneeded morale problems not be caused by implying that these will be the result of implementing a new system. If staff reductions are likely, attrition and early retirement policies should be developed and communicated up front.

Vendor Selection and Contracting

Vendor selection and contracting is a vital step in the systems development process and, if done effectively, helps to minimize the risk of vendor failure. Provider organizations should give extra attention to performing a "due diligence" review of final vendor candidates. This review should include an investigation of the candidates' financial positions, relationships with prior and current customers, and staff mixes. Vendors of emerging technologies should have considerable, ongoing full-time equivalent (FTE) staff committed to research and development, technical problem resolution, integration of the new technology with existing systems, and user support and training. Health care organizations should consider the following steps in evaluating and selecting the best possible vendor:

1. *Determine whether the vendor has a compatible vision of the health care market and of its system's role within that market.* Does the vendor see the system as an integrated piece of a wider vision, or as an added niche functionality designed to capture or maintain market share? Is the technology central to the vendor's future plans, or offered as a sidenote convenience to customers? These evaluations offer important clues as

to the strength of the vendor's current and future commitment to the technology.

2. *Use the contracting process to begin building an ongoing, win-win relationship with the vendor of emerging technologies.* The added risk inherent in emerging technology sometimes puts the provider organization in a position to negotiate favorable contract terms. Organizations agreeing to act as alpha development or beta test sites, or those that regularly host site visits can help the vendor gain wide exposure for its technology. These same organizations may be able to obtain reduced licensing or maintenance fees in return—for providers offering alpha-site support, royalty fees or equity partnerships are possible.

3. *Visit other sites where the candidate vendor's emerging technology is in use, whether the sites are within or outside health care.* Evaluate the extent and success of emerging technology use. Use the opportunity to speak directly with users, getting an "in the trenches" view from people actually involved in the day-to-day use and ongoing operation of the technology.

4. *Carefully document all promised benefits, resource commitments, and timetables from the vendor.* Ensure that critical items are incorporated into the contract. Write acceptance criteria into the contract and the payment plan. Increasingly, provider organizations are choosing to include request-for-proposal (RFP) responses directly in the acquisition contract. Although many vendors ultimately allow this, many stipulate that they must have the opportunity to review responses—after selection, but before contracting. Provider organizations allowing this behavior run the risk of negating the objective nature of the vendor selection process, and providing an incentive to vendors to be less than entirely candid in their initial RFP responses.

5. *Ensure that the supplier has a rigorous quality assurance program, designed to aggressively identify and correct existing problems, as well as to develop future capabilities proactively.* Ask for response time guarantees, as well as the vendor's escalation policies, to ensure that critical issues are addressed rapidly and consistently. Verify the existence and influence of the vendor's user group.

6. *Make plans with the vendor to deal with the possibility of system or technology failure.* Many vendors will agree to place their system source code into escrow—that is, in the hands of a neutral third party—to be released to the provider organization under a set of predefined conditions. These conditions typically are negotiated at system contracting, and may include vendor business failure or discontinuance of support for a product.

System Implementation

The risks of system implementation can best be managed by formulating clear work plans and implementation schedules, allowing more time for tasks than would be usual for equivalent work on implementation of a proven system. The unusually high risks of failure or malfunction require careful structuring of the system and rigorous testing prior to using the system in an operational environment. Technical safeguards, including parallel processing, backup procedures, and system redundancy (having more than one means to perform a required function) can ease the consequences should a system malfunction. In every case, all system users and operators should be well trained in the use of the new system, and instructed as to the procedure for documenting and reporting system errors or other problems.

System Maintenance, Usage, and Development

Implementation and usage risks continue during this phase of the systems life cycle, although ongoing vendor and technical risks become prominent as well. Key activities during this phase are designed to monitor achievement of benefits that were expected in the systems plan and promised during vendor selection.

The ETOG should continue to survey the market, remaining alert to changes in the system's underlying technology; work collaboratively with the vendor to resolve problems and enhance the system; and closely monitor the vendor's performance and financial condition. Changes in responsiveness or service, high executive turnover, large drops in revenue, or loss of prominent client sites by the vendor should trigger an investigation by the provider organization. Provider organizations also should prepare and maintain a contingency plan to deal specifically with risks of vendor failure, abandonment of the technology, and technical obsolescence. The plan (similar to a disaster-recovery plan) should articulate how service will be restored and continued should the system suddenly become unavailable to the organization.

Evaluating ROI: The State of Emerging Technologies

The majority of information systems and technology termed *emerging* in health care offer capabilities in one of three areas: application software technologies, networking and communications technologies, and clinical process technologies. The motivating forces driving technology development in each of these areas are different, as are the associated risks and rewards. The nature of emerging technology is such that this discussion cannot be all-inclusive. Technologies discussed here may fail, or may move into mainstream acceptance by the time this book is printed. However, each technology shares the characteristics of emerging technologies as discussed throughout this chapter.

Application Software Technologies

Application software technologies typically are used in support of enterprise-wide and/or IDS-wide administrative, financial, or (retrospective) clinical activities involving resource use/scheduling, and data collection and analysis.

These applications can include:

- *Expert applications:* More and more frequently, application software suppliers are designing these systems, or incorporating "expert" functionality into existing systems. In whatever form, an expert system uses rules-based processing (if x is true, then do y unless z is present) to model data or perform tasks previously reliant upon the storehouse of knowledge within individual clinicians' or users' brains. A managed care system with expert functionality might model a provider organization's expected reimbursement based on staff FTEs, patient demographics, number of capitated patient lives, and the direct costs of providing care. (Expert applications are discussed more fully in the later section on clinical process technologies.)
- *"Smart" cards:* Widely hailed by health care reform advocates as the future of health care technology, these applications offer large data storage capabilities. To enable this data storage, the card contains its own microprocessor, which also allows on-card programming. Similar to a credit card, when fully developed, smart cards will make a patient's medical record application system independent. Any provider organization with a card reader will be able to access and add financial, clinical, and administrative data to a patient's medical record.

  Today, development efforts have focused on administrative and financial functionality, allowing the upload of administrative patient data, electronic funds transfer, patient insurance, and eligibility data (although a number of vendors are working to include clinical data as well). This technology has yet to prove economically viable, due at least in part to the nomadic nature of the typical U.S. patient population. To fully succeed, the technology has to be widely adopted, allowing for portable data transfer (as patients change caregivers, the data move with them). Early pilots have been limited by geographic and organizational boundaries. As managed care organizations, with their defined and relatively stable patient populations, continue to grow, this technology may offer increasing levels of benefits.
- *Enterprise scheduling:* Enterprise scheduling applications allow the automated scheduling of patients, providers, and other enterprise resources across the full continuum of care. Resources at all levels can be assigned and reassigned automatically, from inpatient to intermediate care to home health and long-term care. These applications offer tremendous potential in resource utilization efficiencies, staff productivity, and patient satisfaction. Through the use of such functionality, patient visits can be processed more effectively, staff and equipment resources can be utilized 'more efficiently, and delays from unexpected equipment or staff shortage can be minimized.
- *Protocol management:* Through the use of large-scale data warehouses and decision support applications, some suppliers offer provider organi-

zations the capability to design, test, and incorporate automated clinical practice protocols into their daily operations. A growing number of decision support system vendors are developing and implementing this functionality, incorporating on-line critical pathway variance alerts and practitioner profiling capabilities.

- *Advanced database technology:* Enormous advances in data storage and manipulation techniques are facilitating development of clinical, financial, and administrative warehouses of information. Providers can use the data from these warehouses to measure risk, clinical outcomes, adherence to accepted protocols, population health, and wellness. Given the growing emphasis on clinical quality and cost control, these tools can be very effective in supporting provider organizations.

  Actuarial databases, incorporating benchmark financial, clinical, and other statistical information from a large set of provider organizations, are increasingly being developed. Upon completion, these databases facilitate benchmark comparisons, allowing health care organizations to measure their performance against a set of comparably equipped and structured organizations.

- *Longitudinal case management:* With the large number of mergers and consolidations occurring throughout the U.S. health care industry, more and more provider organizations have the capability to provide care across the entire continuum, including primary care, hospital inpatient, outpatient, specialty, intermediate, and home care. As this infrastructure falls into place, providers are beginning to explore the possibilities and advantages of longitudinal case management, tracking patients from the very beginning of the care experience along through the point when they exit the care continuum. Case management provides for both cost and clinical benefits, as each provider along the continuum is able to access a problem-based history of the presenting patient and to review tests and treatments provided up to the point they have received the patient for care.

Networking and Communications Technologies

Although local and wide area networks are in use at a multitude of health care facilities, there are some advanced networking and communications functionalities that either remain experimental in nature or are still in the developmental stages. Those technologies include community health networking, telemedicine and telehealth, advanced network technology, the Internet, interface engines, and EDI/all-payer gateways.

Community Health Networking

Community health information networks (CHINs) are regional systems designed to receive and share data from a wide range of providers and organizations, and to facilitate on-line information exchange among providers and payers. With this technology, providers anywhere in the community can access and verify a patient's insurance coverage and benefit limitations. CHINs also support collaborative case management and protocol development. In figure 3-2, the potential stakeholders of a CHIN are identified, together with the data they provide to the network.

Mature CHIN technology may change the community view of medical information. Despite this breakthrough potential, however, the technology is still in its infancy. Current efforts have emphasized incremental local site, on-line access to eligibility and patient history; there has not yet been wide-scale community-oriented, on-line interactive modification of information. Barriers to development of these systems include:

- *The disparity of CHIN cost-benefit distribution among participants:* What level of cost participants will bear and the distribution of financial benefits are key issues with which participants continue to struggle. There is great disparity within communities in terms of the burden that participating organizations are able or willing to accept.
- *The technical limits of wide area networking:* Interconnecting and maintaining links between many disparate, smaller networks requires a group commitment to technical and maintenance staff resources.
- *The availability of electronic payer information:* Currently, few payers are willing or able to either allow widespread access to on-line enrollee information or support broad uses of EDI.
- *The ongoing security and confidentiality of data:* Organizations are rightfully cautious about providing access to sensitive or confidential information.
- *The difficulty in ensuring data standards and integrity:* To date, there are no consistent data standards for medical information. Developing and implementing these standards prior to implementation is critical to CHIN success.

However, regardless of these barriers, employers and payers are forcing the issue, using currently available technology to set up CHINs. Ongoing health care mergers and development of regional health care delivery systems will cause closed, proprietary CHINs to spread. For the next two to three years, CHIN development is likely to emphasize municipal and regional (county-level) sharing of information. Participation in a CHIN may become a requirement of doing business as payers, regulators, and business coalitions demand increased access to on-line financial and clinical information.

Telemedicine and Telehealth

Most commonly seen as the access solution for rural populations, telemedicine and telehealth — the access to and use of medical expertise over

Figure 3-2. Community Health Information Network

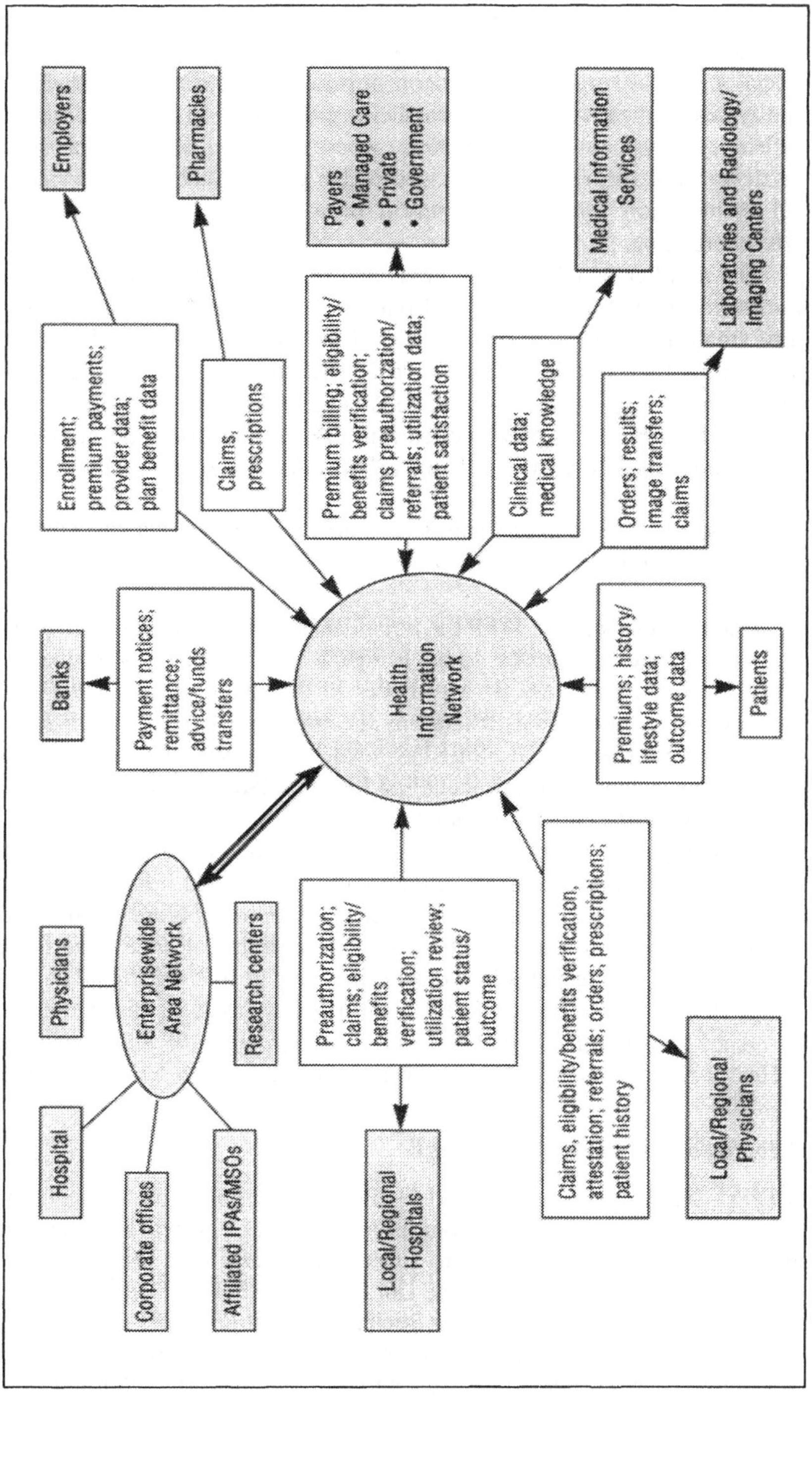

telecommunications lines — offer potential for any population without clear and easy access to medical care. Programs in place offer primary and specialty care to rural groups, prison populations, and those aboard ship. In a typical clinical scenario, telemedicine patients go to a defined location (infirmary, physician office, or clinic) where a trained clinician (physician, physician assistant, registered nurse, or other practitioner) conducts a physical examination under the direction of a physician (or specialist) via teleconferencing.

The number of telemedical programs offering actual interactive communication between physician and patient is increasing, although it is still quite small. In North America, between 1994 and 1995, the number of programs more than doubled, from 10 to 26.[1] In addition to clinical consultations, other key potential uses of telemedicine include teleradiology and imaging, health care provider education, patient education, administrative teleconferencing, procedural demonstrations, and undergraduate and graduate education.

However, a number of formidable cost and legal barriers to telemedicine exist, including:

- *Medical accountability:* With the potential to transcend geographic boundaries, telemedicine raises some licensing and jurisdictional questions providers must address. If a provider in one state treats a patient, via telemedicine, in another, where has the transaction legally occurred? If there is a problem, what court has legal jurisdiction to resolve the matter? Some state legislatures, including Kansas, Texas, and Maine, are beginning to examine these questions.
- *Costs and funding:* The need for rapid transfer of sometimes complicated imagery can require expensive equipment. Federal seed funding for grants and Medicare reimbursement of telemedical pilot programs is uncertain. Four key agencies that fund telemedical programs all face large budget cuts (two of the agencies face discontinuation at this writing). The agencies include the Office of Rural Health Policy (may be eliminated), the Agency for Health Care Policy and Research (may be eliminated), the Health Care Financing Administration, and the Rural Utilities Services.

Advanced Network Technology

Network technologies are used to facilitate communication between computers, often across wide geographic distances. Network design and implementation will be critical to success for health care providers of the future. For the past two years, one-third of HIMSS/HP (Healthcare Information and Management Systems Society/Hewlett Packard) survey respondents have cited "Integration across separate facilities" as their top priority over the next two years.[2] Early adopters of new network technologies will be better able to set up and maintain CHINs and regional information systems linking diverse provider sites.

A number of standards are in use in health care today. The prevailing standard for health care networks is Ethernet; 53 percent of those who responded to the 1996 HIMSS/HP survey plan to use this standard. Other popular standards making headway in health care include asynchronous transfer mode (ATM), fiber distributed data interface (FDDI), wireless LAN (local area network), and fast Ethernet. These technologies are widely present in non–health care environments.

Overall, the basis for realizing full benefits from networking and data communication is preparation and use of an organizational network plan. Success factors include:

- Defining which locations (providers, organizations, and patients) are likely to need to share data.
- Defining the volume and frequency of data access as well as the media to be supported. Requirements for voice- and data-only networks are significantly less than those for multimedia networks, which require high bandwidth as well as increased monitor resolution.
- Using a common network protocol and network vendor for the entire organization. (At the least, compatibility and interoperability should be assured by the vendors.)
- Balancing network cost and capability.

As is typical with emerging technologies, rapid advances are being made in the functionalities and applications of networking technology. This evolution is currently affecting three major areas of networking: data transmission speeds, data safeguards, and global network use and development.

Continued Migration toward 100 MBPS Data Transmission Speeds
At this time, there has been widespread adoption by providers of both the fast Ethernet standard and the FDDI standard. These will both fully support wide area networks (WANs), multimedia graphics applications (such as intensive use of teleradiology), and high levels of data sharing among providers.

Increased Data Safeguards
Mainframe-style disaster recovery capabilities are now possible for network PC-based systems and client/server architectures. New network features support intelligent routing and disaster recovery. Networks can include "mirrored" hard disks inside servers. Data are written simultaneously to multiple hard disks; if the primary disk fails, the second disk comes on-line. The network administrator is warned, but user activity is not disrupted.

"Hot" backup servers can go on-line with a mirror image of the current data, even if the motherboard on the primary server fails. Routers and hubs include the capability of sending network traffic around a failed node or server, and of alerting the network administrator that a problem has occurred. All these features are essential enabling technologies for the movement of mission-critical systems from the mainframe or minicomputer platform to PC- and client/server-based networks.

Global Network Use and Development

Global networking is the ability of health care organizations to use international voice and data networks. Such usage can result in better access to databases as well as international video conferencing. International networks are required for emerging multinational regional care systems (such as West Coast organizations that also serve Mexico, the Pacific Rim, and Asia). For multinational care delivery systems, network use has been limited to exchange of selected data. Voice and video global networks exist now, but are expensive to use. However, these costs are likely to decline. Continued evolution of the global market will result in commercially available, rapid network systems for all technologies. The most common and pervasive example of global networking technology in use today is the Internet.

The Internet

Like few technologies ever have, the Internet has taken health care — and most other industries — by storm. An interconnected "network of networks," the Internet offers users access to information and people around the world. Originally developed by the U.S. Department of Defense, the Internet is now privately administered and used by educational, commercial, and governmental organizations of all types and sizes. In health care, organizations have begun to use the Internet, and the World Wide Web, for a number of purposes, including internal communications, external marketing, access to educational materials, and networking with geographically dispersed colleagues.

The communications potential of the Internet has only begun to be understood; what is clear, however, is that an astonishingly large volume of people in the U.S. and Canada have some kind of access to the Internet. One survey places the number at 37 million people, 17 percent of the total population.[3] Although no health care organization has yet to fully tap the potential of this medium, efforts to do so are clearly under way.

Interface Engines

Interface engines act as bi-directional translators, enabling disparate and incompatible hardware and software applications to freely share data. With communications protocols, they use a low-level translation process to enable hardware connectivity. Once the platforms are connected, the interface engine accepts messages from all involved application systems, performs formatting and editing activities, and then reroutes messages to other systems. Interface engines should take advantage of data standards such as Health Level 7 (HL7). They extend the functionality of data networks because they allow access (within security limits) to any application on the network from any workstation on the network, with a common user interface.

Interface engines offer a number of other benefits, including:

- They preserve existing hardware and software investments by allowing interconnectivity.
- They allow data sharing across the continuum of care.
- They can act as the basis for development of an enterprise data repository, incorporating clinical as well as financial data.

EDI/All-Payer Gateways

EDI, a technology new to the health care industry, uses a single set of communications standards to create a seamless interface, then electronically passes the most common communications among affiliated entities and payers. Typically, these communications include claims submission, remittances, authorizations, and referrals. In some instances, gateways also can serve as a collection point for reporting outcomes, claims, and utilization. Through efficiencies gained, the all-payer gateway can make providers more attractive contracting candidates for payers by reducing costs for both, as well as improving provider ability to track and evaluate the value and worth of contracts.

Clinical Process Technologies

Historically the least automated area of health care, clinical process activities now are the subject of product development by vendors and providers around the world. Oriented toward one or more aspects of clinical patient care, "emerging" clinical technologies include:

- EMR and core supporting technologies (CDRs, clinical workstations)
- Point-of-service and wireless devices
- Expert systems
- Patient imaging and optical devices
- Patient interactive systems
- Interactive voice technology
- Voice data entry and speech recognition

Electronic Medical Record and Core Supporting Technologies

An EMR is more than a computerization of routine patient care or administrative information. Many organizations are working toward some vision of the EMR. When asked to describe their progress toward implementing a computer-based patient record system, only 3 percent of 1996 HIMSS/Hewlett Packard Leadership Survey respondents indicated no plans toward computerization. (See figure 3-3 for full responses.)

In its maturity, the EMR (sometimes called the computer-based patient record) will replace the paper record as the primary method of tracking clinical, financial, and demographic patient information. Together with core supporting technologies such as clinical data repositories (CDRs) and clinical workstations, the EMR eventually will meet the need for real-time data access and evaluation in patient care, creating a completely electronic health record. Figure 3-4 illustrates how the three technologies (the CDRs, EMR, and clinical workstations) interact; the risks and rewards of this technology are addressed in more detail in chapter 4.

Overall, the EMR will provide an electronic, interactive system that care practitioners can access at any point of service, quickly and easily viewing and updating select patient medical data. Those data may include patient

Figure 3-3. HIMSS/Hewlett Packard Leadership Survey Respondents

Describe your progress in implementing a computer-based patient record system.

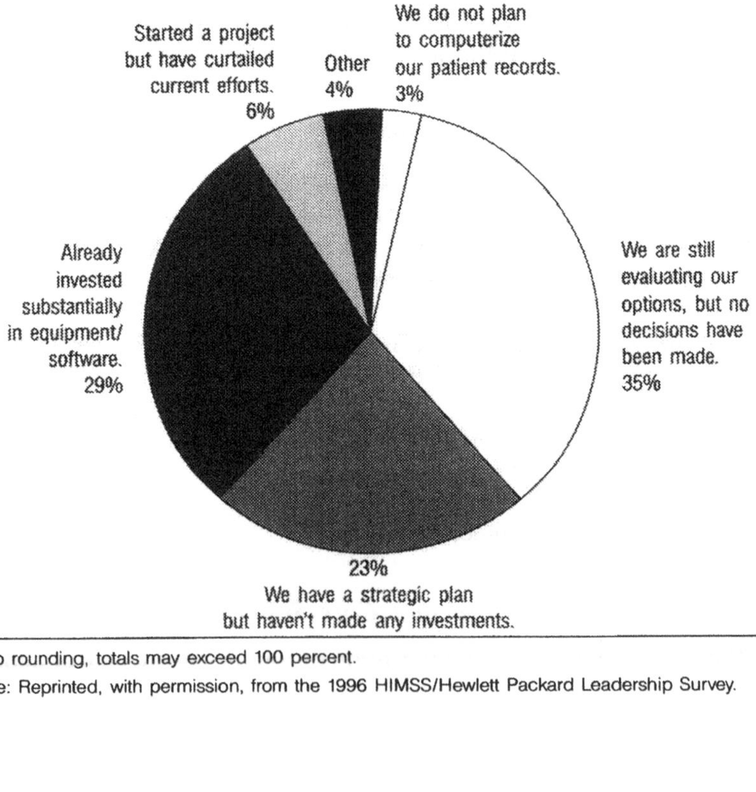

Due to rounding, totals may exceed 100 percent.

Source: Reprinted, with permission, from the 1996 HIMSS/Hewlett Packard Leadership Survey.

Figure 3-4. The Components of the Electronic Medical Record

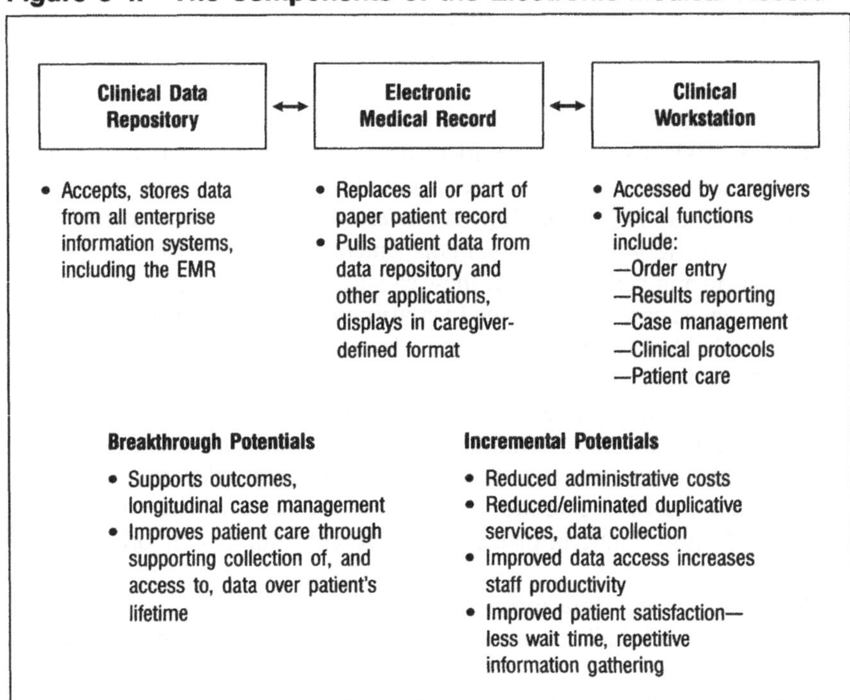

histories, treatment notes and results, laboratory and radiology reports, clinical quality indicators, or health assessment results. This information will be available at one or multiple points of any patient's lifetime—a completely paperless record, contained in electronic format, immediately accessible to those who require the information.

Technical barriers to the EMR are falling, with advances in client/server technology, networks, expert systems, and graphic user interfaces for health care applications. However, there are still barriers relating to laws and practitioner custom. Many states still require manual physician signature of medical records; acceptance of electronic physician signature is limited. Also, many physicians remain unconvinced of the benefits available to them through the use of IT, making clinician education critical in any project involving this technology.

The EMR offers a number of potential incremental benefits, including reduced administrative costs, improved quality of care, and improved convenience and access for patients and care practitioners. Breakthrough benefits come from the EMR's ability to capture rich longitudinal information for evaluation and analysis, supporting outcomes, case management, and clinical quality improvement activities. Although some hospitals and technology suppliers are working toward comprehensive EMRs, fully operational and tested systems do not yet exist. (See chapter 4 for a more in-depth look at the potentials of EMR/CDR technology.)

Clinical Data Repositories

CDRs are databases that hold patient demographic, financial, and clinical information on-line, with department-, enterprise-, and communitywide data access and input. This technology is one essential component of the EMR; on a broader scale, it supports case management and an enterprisewide patient identification number. Because of these capabilities, CDRs support the migration to managed care as well as the formation of regional health care delivery systems. In the 1996 HIMSS/HP survey, 27 percent of respondents cited "implement a clinical data repository" as their most important application priority for the next year (the largest percentage of any technology).

Initial costs for implementation of a clinical data repository may range from $500,000 to $3 million, excluding network and telecommunications costs, depending on the vendor chosen and the scale of the implementation. In addition, CDR implementation raises a number of other issues:

- Data security and data integrity
- Data standards for all systems and organizations supplying or using repository data
- Access workstation technologies and standards

CDRs will support breakthrough gains from implementation of the EMR; short-term, measurable benefits also are possible due to use of information in the data repository to perform concurrent case management, critical path analysis, population "wellness" reviews, and utilization review.

Clinical Workstations

Clinical workstations make up the final critical component for the full implementation and use of an EMR. Typically, workstations use multimedia client/server technology for data management by those providing patient care. Pilot project implementations of this technology are under way at several major providers.

Several hardware and software standards are competing for market position; at this time, UNIX-based workstations are the usual choice. Acceptance of this technology will be enhanced by improved performance and lower prices for servers and workstations. The "networked" hospital will then be feasible; clinical workstations will allow providers to view and analyze data in a way that has been impossible with paper medical records.

Provider organizations interested in this technology should closely monitor the progress, successes, and failures associated with pilot implementation of clinical workstations. Use of this system offers the possibility of breakthrough gains on productivity and proactive patient care management. Incremental benefits are possible by reducing the costs of medication and treatment errors; these improvements can enhance the quality of care while lowering costs.

Clinical Instrumentation

The integration of diagnostic and treatment instruments into the hospital information system is another technology supporting the move toward a "paperless" medical record. The first step has been the acquisition and presentation of information electronically from patient-monitoring devices (for example, in the critical care unit) and other services (for example, monitoring of IV drug delivery systems, home care IV infusion therapy). In the future, these systems may develop into automated patient medical management systems. The only such systems now available are entry level IV mixture calibrations. Current research and development efforts are focused on more effective data transfer, not on fully automated patient management.

Use of direct data acquisition from medical instruments is another supporting technology for the EMR. However, having treatment decisions made by instruments integrated into the health care information system (HIS), without human review and intervention, poses great risks for system failure and harm to patients. Fully automated treatment systems should be approached with great caution. Software and hardware that directly affect the provision of health care without human intervention are subject to stringent Food and Drug Administration (FDA) regulations. The FDA views these systems as "medical devices" similar to X-ray machines or EKGs.

Point-of-Service and Wireless Devices

Point-of-service and wireless devices, allowing caregivers to input and access patient data from the actual point of care delivery, offer potential benefits to productivity as well as care quality. With connections to the CDR, as well as built-in stock phrase "shortcuts" and point-and-click or electronic pen technology, these types of devices can speed care and improve documentation for both nursing and physician staff.

Point-of-service and wireless devices have applications in inpatient and ambulatory as well as home care environments. As the core technologies — pen based, wireless, database, visual programming capabilities, EDI — improve, this technology grows in use and general acceptance.

Devices may utilize a variety of technologies. Some may simply be point-of-care (POC) workstations, positioned at the bedside or examination room. Others may be wireless, mobile devices that move with the caregiver. They may utilize narrow-band radio frequency transmission, diffuse infrared signals, or cellular digital packet data (that break messages into a series of packets, then send the packets along idle or dedicated channels of existing cellular voice networks). Point-of-service devices also may be laptop computers with links into the enterprise network.

The 10 most common mobile medical computing features are:[4]

1. Procedural coding (CPT)
2. Diagnosis coding (ICD9-CM)
3. Subjective objective assessment plan (SOAP) documentation
4. Computerized patient medical record access and update
5. Order drugs and generate prescriptions
6. Order lab tests
7. Order X rays
8. Patient demographic information access and update
9. Generate reports (such as medications, vital signs)
10. Alert to drug interactions

Figure 3-5 shows some of the typical areas in which health care providers are investing in POC technology. Incremental benefits with this technology come primarily from process improvements (such as time savings or improved documentation). The breakthrough potential of POC technology comes from its ability to free clinical staff from location restrictions. Using POC technology, nurses can chart from the patient's room, clinic staff from examination cubicles, and home health staff from patient homes. To date, however, this potential has been frustrated by technical limitations (such as bulky hardware or systems that are difficult or awkward to use).

Expert Systems

Expert systems provide the ability to consolidate a predefined set of rules (from one or more experts) into an application system. These rules then are used to process a unique data set against predetermined variables. Applications in use include medical diagnosis and clinical information systems. Expert systems are increasingly used in administrative and financial applications, such as patient accounts (credit and risk assessment), cash monitoring, and reimbursement control. Artificial intelligence efforts are largely related to "pushing" the expert technology into more intuitive approaches. The premise behind expert technology is being developed and implemented on a smaller scale by software vendors (as discussed earlier in this chapter), with functionality embedded in application systems to support clinical evaluation activities.

Expert systems will continue to proliferate and focus on critical outcome drivers, preemptive quality control, and predictive administrative management systems. Expert systems also will incorporate "prompting systems" to consolidate new learning experiences (possibly through use of knowledge engines that simulate intelligent processes). This ability to "learn"

Figure 3-5. Point-of-Care System Use

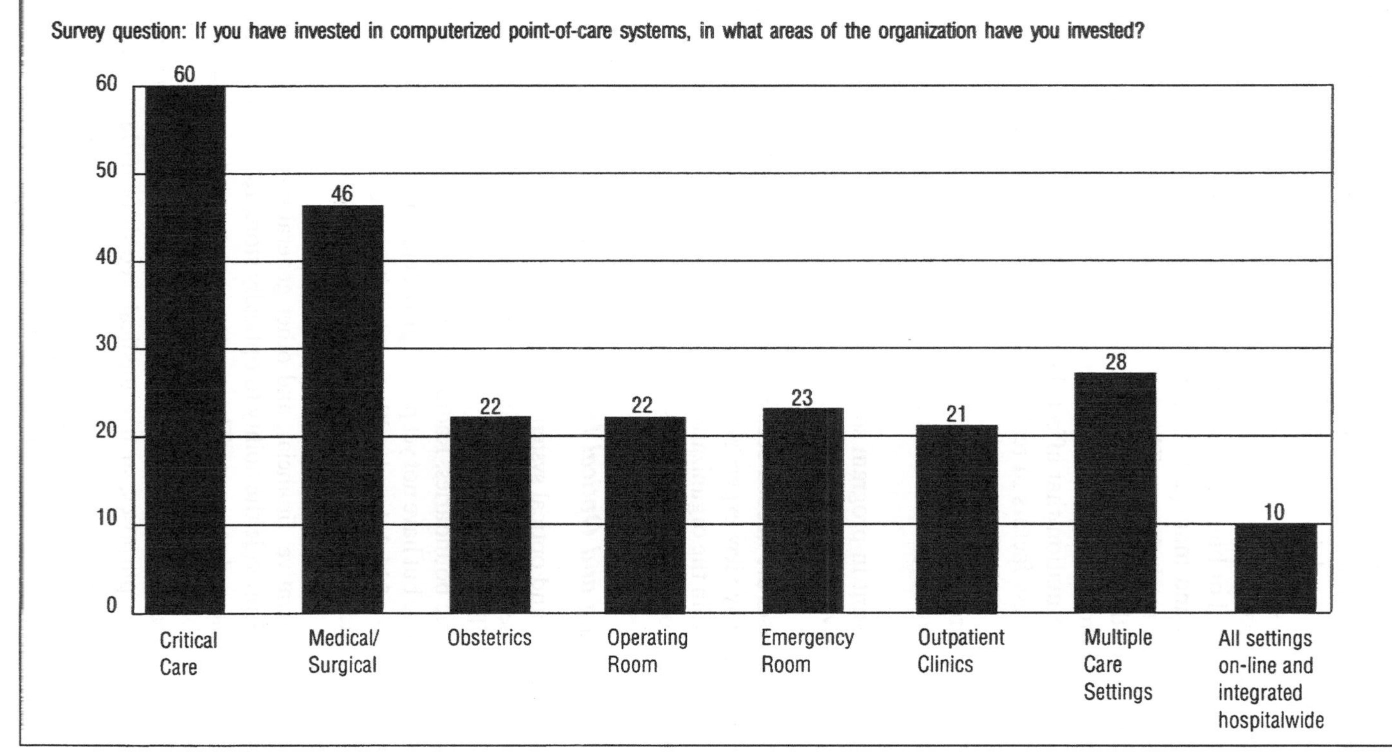

Due to rounding, totals may exceed 100 percent.

Source: Reprinted, with permission, from the 1995 HIMSS/Hewlett Packard Leadership Survey.

from past experiences will allow organizations to more closely monitor and standardize their patient and administrative processes. Pure artificial intelligence — machines capable of equivalent human thought — will remain elusive and undefined; its application will be more powerful, intuitive, easy-to-use expert systems.

The principal benefit that expert systems can deliver, which may be of either incremental or breakthrough value to the provider organization, is to guide providers and managers to a more standardized and well-informed process of making decisions. This will be essential in structured, budget-constrained health care delivery systems. Additionally, expert systems can help managers and providers gain access to and control over the increasing volume of data and information that affect their decisions.

Critical success factors in realizing benefits from expert systems are:

- Careful requirements definition and vendor selection
- Obtaining user "buy-in" that an expert system is necessary and can offer benefits
- User involvement in program selection
- Comprehensive user training

All these processes are needed because users, especially physicians and middle managers, may view expert systems as a threat to their professionalism and position within the organization. Without user acceptance, no program can deliver the benefits its vendors promise.

Patient Imaging and Optical Devices

Patient imaging and optical systems are used commonly to enhance radiology functionalities as well as office automation capabilities. Radiology imaging provides the ability to electronically process and transfer diagnostic images across geographic boundaries. Radiology picture archival systems are commercially available but have not yet passed providers' "price effectiveness test," notably because of high bandwidth and monitor resolution requirements. Investigative and pilot projects have been successful, although wide-scale implementation has yet to occur.

For administrative, financial, and other general business applications, imaging systems provide the ability to optically store, retrieve, and manipulate traditional paper documents. These systems can support corporate libraries and knowledge bases, data distribution by a fax-on-demand system, and long-term storage of paper records in multiple, safe sites. Optical storage and retrieval for administrative purposes, such as medical records or patient accounting, has shown itself to be cost-effective, reducing paper and storage costs (incremental benefits). Today, increasingly flexible indexing schemes are expanding the role of this technology toward breakthrough benefits potential.

Advanced imaging applications today are supporting work flow design and reengineering, electronic physician signature, and moves to EMR technology.

Technical advances in workstations and mass storage will make both imaging and optical technologies mainstream purchases by further reducing cost and increasing performance. Elimination of traditional document storage becomes technically feasible in 1997–1998. At that time, optical storage techniques for administrative applications—with indexing schemes to traditional databases—will become widespread and cost-effective.

Soon, the storage mechanism of choice for both diagnostic radiology and administrative applications will be optical image storage. Concurrent with the clinical workstation revolution, the capability to view and manipulate diagnostic images without film at the clinical workstation will be common and accepted technology.

Optical imaging and retrieval systems should be fully integrated with office automation, financial, and radiology systems in order to deliver the benefits of which the new technology is capable. Integration with optical imaging should be part of the selection criteria for major new systems purchases.

Patient Interactive Systems

Patient interactive systems allow a patient to interact directly with a provider's IS either within a provider facility, at work, or from home by using a personal computer and an appropriate password. The growth of the Internet has spurred increased interest in and use of this type of technology. Patients may use administrative applications to schedule an appointment or verify payment of an account balance. Another application is direct clinical usage, answering on-line questions about symptoms and receiving care instructions based on the individual patient's profile at the provider facility. In total, patient interactive systems give the patient or enrollee access to:

- Appointment schedules
- Pretest regimens
- Health education information
- Medication information
- Account balance and payment information
- Self-diagnosis protocols
- On-line support groups

Several investigative efforts are under way for both administrative and clinical applications. Major efforts are being funded by health plans and health maintenance organizations (HMOs) and relate to appointment scheduling, self-diagnosis and treatment, medication management, and patient education. One system exists that will screen current symptoms against medication profiles, known contraindications, and treatment progress. It will immediately alert the patient's provider if a significant care problem exists; it also will alert the patient to call immediately.

Over the longer term, increases in network bandwidth and the power of microprocessors, as well as advances in medical instrumentation, may support in-home testing and results reporting, vital signs and EKG monitoring, and real-time patient–provider conferences. This can support decentralization of much care that now is provided in medical offices, hospitals, and nursing homes. Indeed, the 21st century may see the return of the house call.

This technology has tremendous potential to revolutionize the "self-care process," facilitated by continued developments in home computing and telecommunications. Current investigative efforts are resulting in implementation for targeted, high-risk populations. On-line patient interactive systems eventually will be a common (though not major) delivery technique. However, usage of these systems will be subject to provider and consumer acceptance.

Patient interactive technologies have the potential to control health care costs by directing patients toward self-care when appropriate or toward the physician's office or hospital when necessary. The breakthrough potential for improved patient education and lifestyle management is extremely large. Payers can expect decreased long-term costs through increased wellness of enrolled populations. Providers can anticipate an increased ability to utilize home care services. The incremental potential for the provider includes a decrease in staff burdens and overtime, an improvement in productivity, and the ability to handle increased patient volume.

This technology is likely to be widely accepted by patients, as home computer use spreads and as patient desire for information and involvement in the treatment process increases. Ongoing trends toward longer workweeks also will foster patient demand for this technology and any other that permits them to meet their needs more rapidly. Therefore, adoption of patient interactive technology can provide economic and market position advantages to health care organizations. With phased implementation of these systems, organizations can learn from their providers' and patients' experience, as well as from the experience of other organizations.

Interactive Voice Technology

In health care, interactive voice technologies are taking advantage of the common and widespread use of the telephone to facilitate a number of common health care activities such as time reporting, patient education, and staff scheduling. Through a series of voice prompts, interactive voice technology users can report or verify their work schedules, access recording information about a particular illness or procedure, or submit a request for paid time off.

The near-universal acceptance of the telephone allows this technology to avoid some of the user risks prevalent with other types of technology.

As provider organizations struggle with increasing patient volumes and decreasing resources, some organizations have begun to explore the use of interactive voice technology to supplement existing staff. Pilot projects, using interactive voice technology to facilitate patient scheduling, provide automated testing and procedure information, and provide community members with information on basic health topics, have proved successful in some communities. Other facilities have taken advantage of interactive voice technology to collect employee time and attendance information, decreasing the administrative reporting burden on payroll staff and employees.

Voice Data Entry and Speech Recognition

Voice data-entry and speech recognition technologies began, at least in part, from the legendary physician resistance to typing. Two levels of systems have evolved: One type acts primarily as a voice recorder/dictation system allowing physicians to enter verbal notes for later transcription or permanent voice storage into the patient record. The other type of system, using voice recognition, actually translates the practitioner's speech into commands or free text.

Up-to-date, investigative efforts have been very limited and modest in success, with primary emphasis on voice-to-text transcription. Refinement of this technology is continuing; although without further technical breakthroughs, it is doubtful that language and usage barriers will allow use beyond a limited word set. Efforts will likely stay focused on select voice-to-text applications and limited voice-command applications.

Looking Forward

Through utilizing the comprehensive approach discussed in this chapter—investigation, evaluation, planning, implementation, and reevaluation—health care provider organizations stand to gain tremendous benefits from the use of emerging technologies. Although it should be emphasized that it is impossible to fully contain the risks inherent in these investments, in most cases risk can be held to a manageable level.

Not every technology listed here will gain full acceptance in the health care industry—some will fail, some will gain only moderate use in the mainstream of provider organizations. Other technologies, not yet envisioned, will come forward. Each one was developed to meet an existing provider need, real or imagined. Over time, those technologies that do succeed will have been proven not only cost-effective, but also to offer added value to the direct delivery of health care. Establishing a framework within which to measure that value positions provider organizations to take full advantage of still-evolving technologies.

References

1. Allen, A., and Allen, D. Telemedicine programs: 2nd annual review reveals doubling of programs in a year. *Telemedicine Today* 3(2):1, Spring 1995.

2. The HIMSS/Hewlett Packard Leadership Survey. Chicago: Health Care Information and Management Systems Society, 1995 and 1996.

3. The CommerceNet/Nielsen Internet Demographics Survey. San Francisco and New York City: CommerceNet and Nielsen Media Research, 1995.

4. Grimm, C. B. Mobilizing physicians for wireless technology. *Healthcare Informatics* 12(1):70–74, Jan. 1995.

The Long-Range Plan: A Model for Maximum Returns

Attaining quantified benefits from health care information technology (IT) is an important goal for every organization — but it should not be the complete focus of the information life cycle. IT programs and investments must be balanced against many other factors, including the surrounding market, the management team's coherence and interaction, and the development stage of the health system. To fully succeed, all key IT decisions and requirements must be brought into a centralized planning framework, with identified and measurable goals and objectives.

The easiest and most structured mechanism that can be used to create this framework is a formal long-range plan (LRP). An LRP is a management tool providing a strategic and operational blueprint for the time span it addresses (typically 3 to 5 years). Represented in the LRP is a convergence of the organization's IT history, current capabilities, new architectural directions, technology, affordability, and system installation sequencing. The LRP operationalizes the organization's philosophy toward the appropriateness of, and balance between, breakthrough and incremental return expectations. The first two to three years of the plan are relatively precise; the final years of coverage are more visionary in nature, subject to the vagaries of market activity, hardware/software costs, management direction, local market evolution, and constituent interests. (An example of a portion of a strategic long-range plan, along with a table of contents of a full plan, is presented later in the chapter.)

Long-range planning is never a static process. It presents senior and executive management the opportunity to identify and evaluate the true goals and direction of the organization from a business perspective. Establishing key guidelines and activities can ensure that a high-quality level of thought and consideration is incorporated into the process, although true strategists will always leave room for the unexpected. It is interesting to note that IT failure is attributed more often to management and planning problems than to actual technology failure.

The LRP document creates harmony between IT and enterprise goals, substantiating the critical importance of existing and ongoing IT initiatives.

That difficult goal, when coupled with the potential life and death nature of health care provision, creates tremendous pressure for all encompassing, insightful planning. With such momentous weight placed on LRP development, and with the complexities inherent in creating such a plan, many management teams are intimidated by the whole idea of long-range planning. In many cases, IT managers find it easier to focus on the budget-related aspects of long-range planning than on using the plan to challenge the organization to greater heights.

To this point, this book has concentrated on discrete parts of the long-range planning process: forming expectations and strategy, evaluating the risks and rewards of alternatives, and identifying realistic benefits of IT investments. This chapter draws these activities together into the framework for a formal LRP. Specific discussion topics include:

- How benefits orientation and return-on-investment (ROI) expectations fit into the long-range planning process
- What a full information systems (IS) five-year plan might look like
- How that plan might be adopted to detail a smaller-scale or "at-risk" project, such as implementation of an enterprise electronic medical record (EMR) and clinical data repository (CDR)

Compiling the Long-Range Plan

As illustrated in figure 4-1, the path to a formal LRP incorporates many of the activities discussed throughout this book. Although analysis and evaluation of alternative technologies are ongoing, educating the organization on the importance and benefits of information technology is critical. No LRP will succeed without the support and validation of IT staff, organizational management, and IT end users.

In general terms, the LRP should:

- Identify how technology will effectively support overall strategic goals
- Evaluate the organization's current IT strengths and weaknesses in support of overall goals
- Incorporate organizational needs, both real and perceived
- Review systems needs of the enterprise as a whole, rather than individual departments
- Generate organizationwide support and involvement in planning
- Facilitate the view of information as an organizational resource, rather than one "owned" by a particular department or entity
- Determine IS affordability and priorities

Figure 4-1. Long-Range Systems Planning

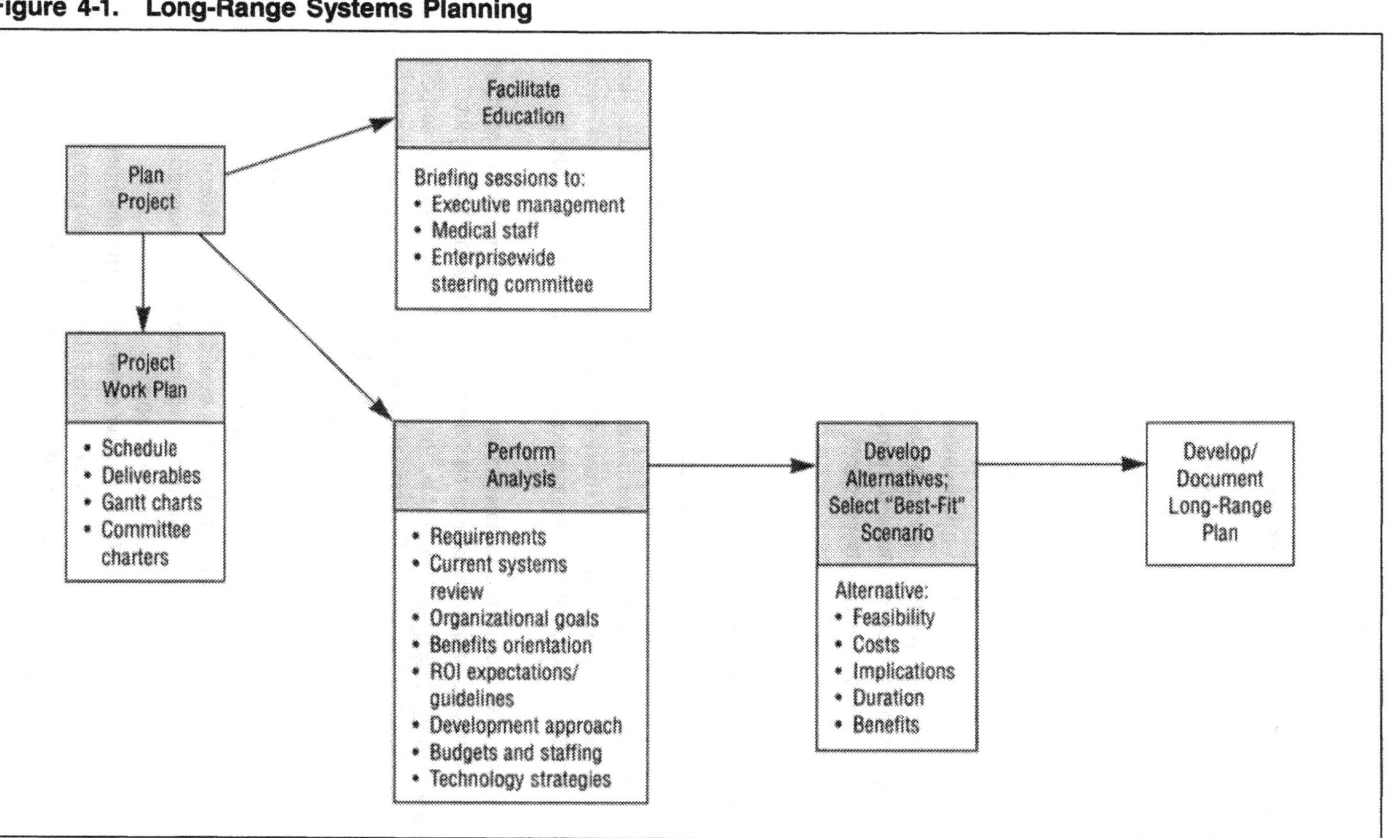

Creating the Formal Planning Document

In a formal LRP, individual sections present a balance of strategic and operational planning. This presentation is designed to clearly articulate both the short- and long-term steps that an organization will take to meet the overall IT vision and to support overall organizational goals. The LRP is composed of nine sections, each with a distinct purpose and containing specific information:

1. Executive summary
2. Planning methodology
3. Current status of information systems
4. Information systems direction
5. Information systems implementation
6. Information systems cost projections
7. Information systems benefit projections
8. Information systems department requirements
9. Appendixes

Executive Summary

As a rule, health care executives are ferociously impatient readers, typically with little time to spend reviewing written documents. A formal LRP should never be issued without this brief introductory section highlighting key decisions, strategies, and benefits. This document, particularly useful for board-level review, should include a number of subsections, including:

- *Preface:* A brief introduction to the LRP, identifying key people involved in planning, and describing the motivation behind the project.
- *Direction:* An overview of the "vision" established for the use of IT at the organization, including critical application requirements and specific actualization strategies. This section should emphasize the alignment between organizational business/medical service objectives and the planned information technology.
- *Major recommendations:* An outline of the major recommendations contained in the plan, with a short explanation of the importance of each.
- *Benefits:* A brief listing of the key benefits expected from implementation of the plan. These should be prioritized and presented according to their importance to the organization.
- *Implementation plan:* An overview of the plan that has been established to carry out the recommendations in the LRP. Without going into tremendous detail, this section should discuss timing of implementation, expected resource utilization, and intensity.

- *Investment required and ROI analysis:* A summary of the financial effects, both positive and negative, the plan is expected to provide. The ROI analysis should highlight financial expectations that are fully quantified, as opposed to those that are qualified (and estimated).

Planning Methodology

This section describes the methodology used to arrive at the decisions and conclusions contained in the LRP. Key objectives and steps taken during the planning process should be highlighted, together with the actual time lines followed throughout the project. This section is important because it documents the goals, assumptions, and activities incorporated into the LRP. It also enables those individuals reviewing the LRP to get a complete picture of the planning engagement and provides future planners with a jump-off point for designing new initiatives. Subsections include:

- *Planning goals:* A contextual placement of the planning project, including its scope (for example, full-fledged LRP, at-risk emerging technology) and underlying drivers (for example, five-year plan update, plan for merger/ acquisition)
- *Planning techniques:* Amount and scale of participation from within the organization (for example, primarily committee consensus, IS staff developed with CEO oversight, extended use of physician committees); assumptions made during process (for example, budget increases/decreases, technology availability)

Current Status of Information Systems

This section provides clear documentation of an organization's current IT program (including systems architecture, applications, and technologies in place) or program in the process of implementation. In assembling this concrete benchmark of where an organization stands relative to technology, planners can compare the past and present, formulating a bridge to move from one to the other. Subsections include:

- *History of organizational IT use,* including any large-scale projects or "vision" the organization has worked (or is working) to achieve
- *Architecture overview of in-place systems and networks,* including notation of any ongoing implementation efforts, with projected end dates
- *User perceptions of information systems, technologies, and IS staff,* including whether users feel current systems are adequately meeting needs and how IS department initiatives are typically received by the user population
- *Cost analysis and benchmarking,* including the current utility of in-place systems (the cost efficiency with which they are being used), as well as

the internal and external financial forces (budgets, unavoidable capital expenditures, regulatory compliance requirements) affecting existing IS support for organizational goals and objectives

Information Systems Direction

Throughout the course of long-range planning, various alternative approaches to achieving IS goals are described and considered. In the final LRP document, this section explains how the selected strategy, technical architecture, and specific enabling substrategies address short- and long-term organizational needs. Subsections include:

- *Medical service–business objectives alignment:* How the planned information technology supports the overall goals of the health care organization.
- *Vision, architecture, and development approach:* The organization's "vision" for technology, the technological architecture that is to be employed (technical as well as application), as well as the general approach to be taken in developing the final structure (for example, progression over a period of time, critical issues and strategies).
- *Application requirements:* The purpose of this section is *not* to create or prepare a request for proposal (RFP). Rather, it is intended as an overview portfolio of required applications to support long-range goals and objectives. The portfolio review should include, as appropriate, a comprehensive listing of the types of applications required, including: administrative, clinical, decision support, EMR/CDR, financial, telecommunications, managed care, other specialty/extended care, physician practice, health plan/third-party administrative systems.
- *Specific strategies:* These include, as appropriate, sections relating to networks (wide and local area), database, user access, integration, community health information network (CHIN), workstation (universal, clinical, administrative), electronic data interchange (EDI), PC support tools, and security and data integrity.
- *Data ownership and access policies:* Formal statement of organization's policies toward access of data by nonowned entities (as in when organization is member of a CHIN or participates in regional joint ventures). In some cases, this section may be an affirmative statement regarding the importance of data security, with a projected time frame for development of formal policies.

Information Systems Implementation

This section focuses on the practical time requirements for implementing the technology detailed in the LRP. Both the end vision and the evolution over time are documented. Subsections include:

- *Schedule time line:* An overall time frame to support the full and complete implementation of systems and technologies presented in the LRP. This time frame focuses on identifying and sequencing each technology required by the LRP. In particularly complex or difficult projects, education and change management processes may be included as discrete components.
- *Annual goals:* A year-by-year illustration, often graphical, of the progression toward the LRP vision. This subsection includes figures showing both the architecture and application changes over time (for example, telecommunications upgrade year 1; wide area network up and running in year 2; enterprise scheduling implemented year 3, and so on).

Information Systems Cost Projections

Market factors will always affect the accuracy of cost projections. For the first 2 to 3 years covered by the LRP, numbers will be relatively precise. Years 3 and 4 will be approximations; beyond year 4, all figures will be order of magnitude, reflecting changing priorities and technologies. Nevertheless, the projections need to provide budgetary guidance for the period covered in the LRP. When the LRP incorporates projects with emerging or at-risk technologies, calculating precise figures becomes even more difficult. (Chapter 3 discusses methods and considerations for managing emerging technology projects.) This section's subsections are commonly presented in spreadsheet format, and include:

- *Capital costs,* including items such as new or upgraded hardware and required facilities modifications. In some cases, organizations are capitalizing consulting fees in order to avoid a large initial operating expenditure (although such an action increases depreciation costs, inflating operating expenses for a longer period of time).
- *Operations costs,* which covers noncapital costs, excepting personnel and training (broken out as separate categories). Annual maintenance expenditures (software and hardware) are covered here, as are depreciation and consulting fees.
- *Personnel costs,* detailing expected personnel costs for the life of the plan, including growth and shrinkage.
- *Training costs,* including projections for IS staff as well as end users.

Information Systems Benefit Projections

Through processes detailed in this book, a list of projected benefits is compiled and included in the final LRP. More than a composite listing of potential benefits, this section addresses the ROI analysis methodology, benefits attainment strategies and guidelines, and benefit measurement mechanisms. Subsections include:

- *Strategic:* Those benefits that better position the organization to achieve key business and medical service goals. They may relate to market share, quality of care, or other areas difficult to quantify.
- *Quantified:* Those benefits resulting in actual, documentable impact on an organization's bottom line. They may include reduced overtime costs, improved cash flow, reductions in data-entry redundancy, and so on.
- *ROI analysis and expectations:* A summary review of the expected key benefits from implementing the LRP, including financial and operational benefits.
- *Attainment strategy and guidelines:* Lays out critical strategies geared toward attaining the benefits articulated in earlier subsections. These strategies may relate to things such as applications (for example, organization's attitude toward customized software) or vendors (for example, alpha- or beta-site relationships with technology developers).

Information Systems Department Requirements

The final part of the main body of the report details staffing levels and lines of responsibility. Projected IS staff requirements to effectively implement the long-range plan are identified. Subsections include:

- *Governance:* Details, often through an organizational chart, oversight of information technology at the organization, including the chief IT executive, any existing Information Systems Steering Committee (ISSC) or emerging technology oversight group (ETOG), IS personnel, any existing subgroups within IS (such as quality action teams charged with implementing or monitoring continuous quality improvement [CQI] activities).
- *Organization:* Functional in nature, this chart details the relationships within the IS department, including major divisions and subdivisions (such as customer services, project development, production).
- *Training plan:* This section includes both end-user and IS staff training requirements, opportunities, and program implementation plans. Budget projections in this section consider IS staff training costs, and often "train the trainer" financial commitments required for planned and in-place systems.
- *Skill-mix requirements and plan:* Addresses the IS skill requirements to effectively carry out the recommendations within the LRP. This subsection also would include a discussion of any existing deficiencies in skill mix or resource utilization (many organizations face a shortage of staff to appropriately address end-user requests).
- *Customer delivery system role and structure:* This subsection addresses issues surrounding IS end-user support, including help desk functions, disaster planning/rapid response, and facility representation.

- *Other recommendations:* This final section considers any recommendations not easily categorized elsewhere. For example, it may document a current or expected "gap" in IS department capabilities (such as a lack of experience in disaster planning).

Appendixes

Additional materials, normally developed during the course of the planning engagement, are included to support the objectives, decisions, and recommendations made in the LRP. The conclusions often are a part of the formal LRP document, but the documents are included as addenda or by reference to help manage the size of the LRP. Appendixes might include supporting documents, reports, and work papers such as:

- *Business objectives and systems implications matrix:* An objective-by-objective illustration of the IT implications of each organizational business and medical service objective. (For example, an organization attempting to provide a seamless continuum of care services faces networking and application implications of multiple, disparate facilities.)
- *Requirements report:* This planning document details the specific technology and application needs of an organization through an analysis of current systems, business needs, available resources, and technologies. This report forms the beginning of any RFPs that are to be issued.
- *Specific cost-benefit studies:* Any specific studies carried out or commissioned by the organization that support (or affect) the conclusions and recommendations of the LRP.

Adapting the Plan to Support Emerging or At-Risk Projects

Often organizations embarking on large-scale IT projects, particularly those with enterprisewide implications or those using emerging or other at-risk technologies, will use a scaled-down version of the formal long-range plan to document project strategy and expected returns. The remainder of this chapter illustrates what such a plan might look like. Based on work at Sharp HealthCare, in San Diego, the plan studies the implementation and use of an enterprisewide electronic medical record and clinical data repository.

Sharp HealthCare, a regional delivery network, serves metropolitan San Diego and southern Riverside County. Nearly 30 percent of the 3 million area inhabitants look to Sharp for their health care needs. The Sharp network, with 1,972 licensed beds systemwide, has an outpatient/skilled nursing visit volume of nearly 1.8 million per year. Numerous disparate facilities are included in the network, including:

- Six acute care hospitals
- Three affiliated medical groups with numerous clinics and approximately 2,000 physicians
- Five skilled nursing facilities
- A health plan responsible for approximately 300,000 covered lives
- Numerous specialty organizations including a home health organization, a sports medicine facility, a surgery center, and a wellness center

In February 1995, Sharp HealthCare chartered the Electronic Medical Record and Clinical Data Repository Steering Committee. With support from JDA, the committee acted as the executive and decision-making body for the EMR/CDR project. Its feasibility report was issued in the fall of 1995! Two key findings emerged from the feasibility study:

- To fully exploit EMR/CDR technology, networking and IS interface/integration capabilities must be established and operational. These infrastructure costs return a number of benefits not directly related to EMR/CDR technology—costs are, however, immediate and large.
- At the same time, quantifiable benefit returns do not fully manifest until late in the project time line. Should Sharp adopt the full plan and make the large upfront investments, there would be no assurance of a net positive ROI for the immediate future.

Although Sharp remains committed to the vision and goals behind the enterprise EMR/CDR, the skewed investment/benefit chronology has moved it to adapt a staged investment approach, implementing technology in support of the EMR/CDR as it becomes generally available and proves technically and financially feasible.

The excerpted LRP that follows is based on discussions, activities, plans, and documentation generated and debated over the course of the EMR/CDR feasibility project. The sample plan focuses on three sections from a formal LRP that were chosen to illustrate the critical interconnections between business and technology planning, and benefits projection and realization:

- The executive summary
- Information systems direction
- Information systems cost, benefit, and ROI projections

Each section follows the general formats described previously in the chapter, although they have been customized to meet the specific needs and concerns of the provider organization.

An Example of a Strategic Long-Range Plan*

Strategic Long-Range Plan: Sample Table of Contents

Executive Summary
  Preface
  Overview of direction
  Summary of major recommendations
  Summary of benefits
  Summary of implementation plan
  Summary of investment required and ROI analysis
Information Systems Direction
  Medical service–business objectives alignment
  Vision, architecture, and development approach
  Application requirements
    Administrative
    Clinical
    Decision support
    Electronic medical record/clinical data repository
    Financial
    Telecommunications
    Managed care
    Other specialty/extended care
    Physician practice
    Health plan/third-party administrative systems
  Specific strategies
    Network (wide and local area networks)
    Database
    User access
    Integration
    Community health information network (CHIN)
    Workstation (universal, clinical, administrative)
    Electronic data interchange (EDI)
    PC support tools
    Security and data integrity
  Data ownership and access policies
Information Systems Benefits Projection
  Strategic
  Quantified
    Benefits for Sharp HealthCare Patients
    Benefits for Sharp HealthCare Physicians and Other Providers
    Benefits for the Sharp HealthCare Enterprise and Administration
  ROI analysis and expectations
  Attainment strategy and guidelines
    EMR/CDR Implementation
    Applications
    Vendor
    Project management

---

*"Toward an Enterprise-Wide Electronic Medical Record/Clinical Data Repository." This excerpt was reprinted with permission of Sharp HealthCare, San Diego.

Executive Summary

Preface

The Sharp HealthCare Electronic Medical Record and Clinical Data Repository (EMR/CDR) Steering Committee included membership representing the system, institutional, and community arms of Sharp HealthCare. It was chartered to fulfill five goals:

1. To identify user needs, and to link those needs with opportunities in innovation and technology
2. To assess the feasibility of an enterprisewide electronic medical record (EMR)/ clinical data repository (CDR)
3. To determine critical success factors
4. To identify organizational considerations
5. To develop design alternatives and determine the best fit for Sharp HealthCare

The committee assessed feasibility and implementation requirements through the process illustrated in figure 4-2.

This report details long-term goals, costs, strategies, and benefits expected of and from investment in an enterprisewide EMR/CDR. Goals, objectives, issues, and requirements documented within this report were gathered from both primary and secondary research sources, including existing Sharp HealthCare documentation and studies, staff and management interviews, and cross-organizational benchmarking.

Overview of Direction

Sharp HealthCare considers the need for information distribution and management as critical to long-term organizational health. To facilitate enterprisewide information access, Sharp HealthCare must develop a database and systems strategy that facilitates information exchange with flexibility and without unnecessary restriction. Staff and clinicians have identified the electronic medical record as a critical technology to the continued support of information management and integrated patient services.

As envisioned, the Sharp EMR is enterprisewide in scope, incorporating all clinical constituencies (nurses, physicians, ancillary technicians, case managers, managed care medical directors). Predominantly created on the computer, the EMR is a milestone change from paper-based record keeping, offering user benefits relating to automated data storage, manipulation, and presentation. The EMR supports staff across the continuum of care in accessing valid, reliable, and consistent patient information, regardless of the patient's point of entry into the health network. Table 4-1 illustrates the progression from paper-based medical record to EMR.

The Sharp CDR, working in conjunction with the EMR, would accept data from feeder and legacy systems through an interface engine. CDR data could be accessed

Figure 4-2. Steering Committee Process

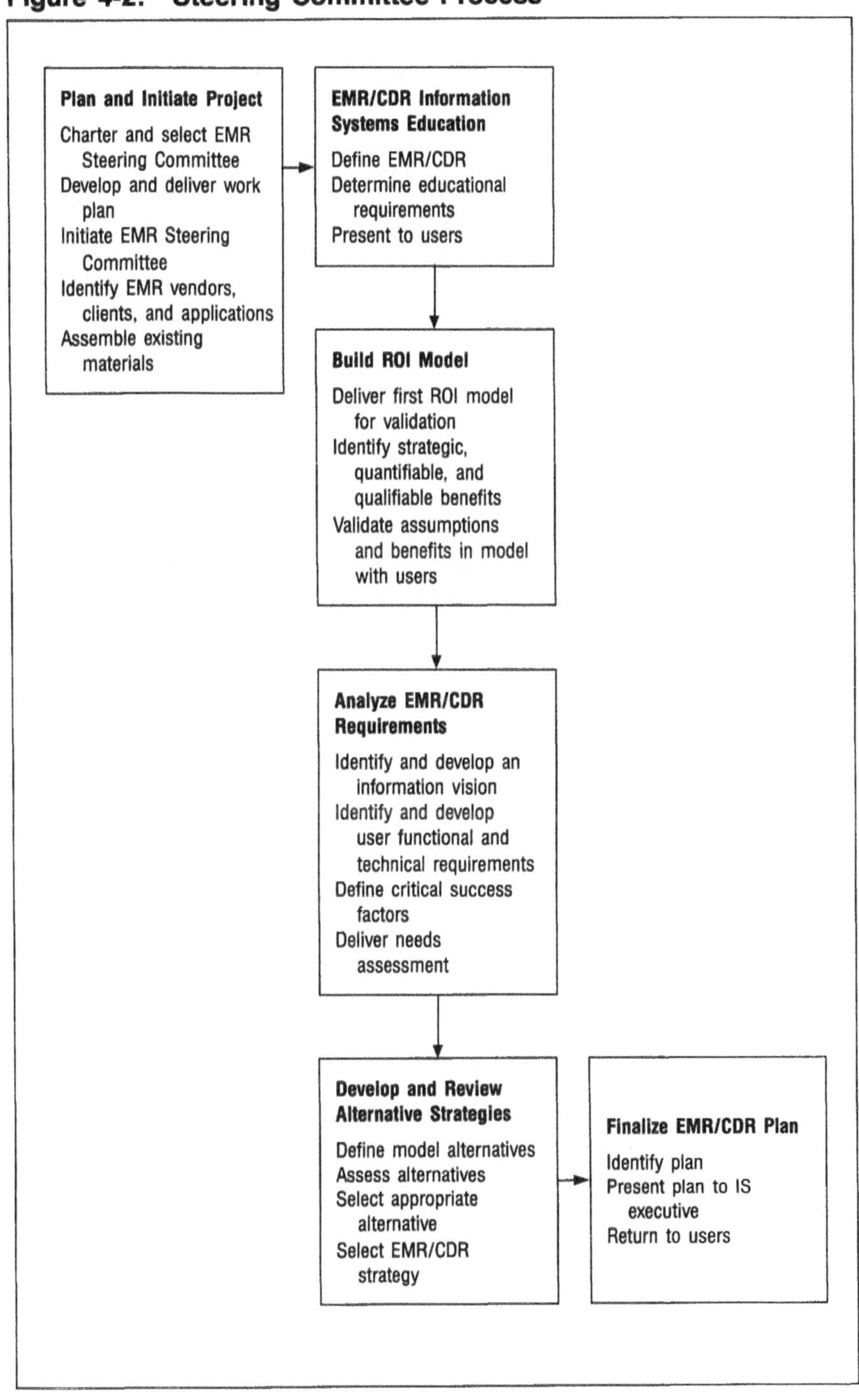

Table 4-1.   Medical Record Format Progression

	Traditional →	Transitional →	Resultant
Type	**Paper Chart**	**Computerized Medical Record (CMR)**	**Electronic Medical Record (EMR)**
Definition	All parts of the chart appear on paper. There may be multiple paper charts for each patient at various locations, including physician offices, clinics, and hospitals.	Achieved by using paper documents and images and converting them into computer format (which may include scanning).	Created on the computer with appropriate software from various sources and data-entry mechanisms, including keyboard, mouse, light pen, touch screen.
At SHARP	Paper charts generated manually or electronically. Charts may exist in several areas within the enterprise for each patient, although patient identifier is unique across the enterprise.	Various automated systems within the SHARP enterprise with various levels of integration. Overall, this has not been used as an intermediary step to the EMR by Sharp HealthCare.	Does not yet exist; subject of study and planning.

by system users with appropriate "views" of data by type and user. The CDR manages data access and security, maintaining data integrity and supporting data backup and recovery. Select information from the enterprise CDR could be transferred to a regional and/or national CHIN for community health management and research needs.

Through the use of EMR/CDR technology, enterprise patient data can be viewed longitudinally, across multiple episodes and/or encounters. It may also be viewed across patients based upon predefined criteria, facilitating enterprise outcome measurements and standardized care plans/protocols.

Summary of Major Recommendations

- Implement phase one of the EMR/CDR long-range plan immediately. In 18 to 24 months, evaluate the functionality of existing systems, then decide if an off-the-shelf product will meet Sharp HealthCare technology requirements. If so, implement phases two through four. By selecting this option, Sharp minimizes development costs and maintains tighter control on the costs of implementation and user training.
- Redefine the EMR SC role to include monitoring and oversight of EMR-related projects. The EMR Steering Committee can play a vital facilitative role in designing, implementing, and monitoring the staff and physician educational process.

At the end of each phase, the committee could review progress and make recommendations for continuance. The committee could be responsible for program oversight, supporting focused evaluation of technology and other forces impacting the EMR/CDR plan.

Summary of Benefits

Throughout the course of the project, the steering committee considered various benefits and the stakeholders who would secure them. The final list of benefits is drawn from 120 user interviews and 250 physician surveys. The key benefits of a patient-centered, enterprisewide data architecture will be:

- Increased data completeness and accuracy through standardized formats and contexts
- Enhanced service and access efficiency through significantly reduced access delays to pertinent care information
- Supported collection of comprehensive, enterprisewide information, throughout all care venues
- Significantly reduced data storage, data management, and data-entry redundancies

The anticipated benefits of EMR/CDR implementation are described in further detail later in this report.

Summary of Implementation Plan

The EMR/CDR implementation strategy has four phases (described in table 4-2) that can be completed in five years with an aggressive Sharp commitment. The end of each phase represents a critical juncture where Sharp HealthCare has an opportunity to evaluate market forces and technology/functionality value of the evolving EMR. Implementation objectives include:

- To provide integrated functionality to all areas of the Sharp HealthCare organization over the long term
- To preserve and enhance a single, enterprisewide master patient index
- To provide users with new or enhanced functionality in the near term, even before all aspects of EMR/CDR technology mature
- To allow extension or expansion of the implementation plan with little risk to previous systems investments
- To provide education to users that details their purpose and role in information management
- To ensure patient and provider confidentiality

The Sharp HealthCare information architecture, as it would stand at the end of phase I, is depicted in figure 4-3.

Summary of Investment Required and ROI Analysis

As noted in the return on investment model presented in table 4-3, Sharp Health-Care must commit significant investment dollars to fully install and realize the benefits of an enterprise EMR/CDR. Full implementation of all phases is an aggressive plan, and assumes no resource limitations. It is important to note that these costs represent total costs, and depending on the actual implementation of the EMR, may vary. Some of the costs described may, in whole or in part, be included in the information systems budget. These costs (and associated economic benefits) are described in more detail later in this report. Key economic implications include:

- Projected benefits of EMR/CDR implementation are approximately $82,529,000. This includes anticipated increases in revenues and membership, and decreases in operating costs due to the use of the EMR/CDR.

Table 4-2. Phases of Implementation

Phase I Years 1 and 2	Phase II Year 3	Phase III Year 4	Phase IV Year 5
Objective: Expansion and stabilization	**Objective: Evaluation and further design**	**Objective: Implementation**	**Objective: Advanced functionality**
• Complete implementation of on-line transcription • Complete IDX-laboratory system interface • Extend IDX functionality to areas not currently served • Conduct training for staff and physicians on current systems • Educate staff and physicians on benefits and effective use of EMR/CDR • Expand implementation of interface engine • Continue application of enterprisewide shared master patient index (MPI) • Complete interface and implementation of pharmacy and home health clinical systems	• Issue the five-year plan for information systems • Complete implementation of enterprisewide-shared MPI • Complete interfaces to other Sharp HealthCare systems, as needed • Complete interface engine implementation • Establish enterprisewide standards for EDI, data definition, reporting and maintenance of system integrity and security • Initiate design of the EMR/CDR	• Complete design of the EMR/CDR • Implement a prototype EMR/CDR as soon as feeder systems are implemented and stable • Provide end-user training for users of prototype system • Implement outcomes measurement and analysis system • Design clinical protocols and critical paths in the EMR/CDR for the continuum of care	• Implement electronic data interchange (EDI) for the enterprise as a whole • Establish retail pharmacy profile interchange • Refine outcomes measurement and analysis; implement changes • Implement use of on-line clinical protocols and critical paths for the continuum of care • Implement expert or rules-based logical components

Figure 4-3. Sharp HealthCare Information Architecture (Phase I)

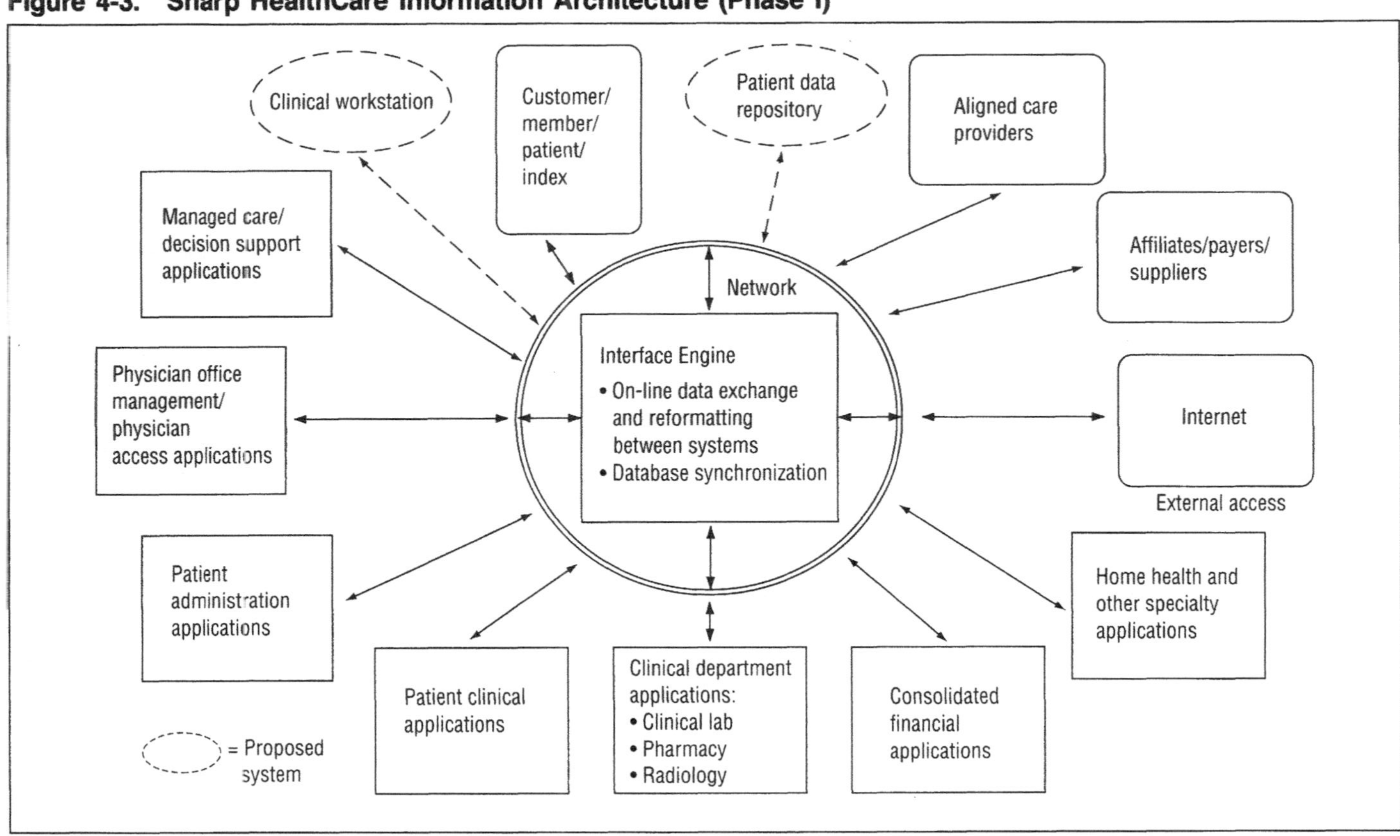

Table 4-3. Sharp HealthCare ROI Model

Benefits		1996	1997	1998	1999	2000	Five-Year Total
	Increased revenues	21,000	210,000	526,000	737,000	895,000	2,389,000
	Decreased costs	638,000	6,583,000	17,570,000	25,120,000	31,346,000	81,257,000
	Architecture benefit adjustment	−9,000	−93,000	−239,000	−345,000	−431,000	−1,117,000
	Total Benefits	650,000	6,700,000	17,857,000	25,512,000	31,810,000	82,529,000
Costs		1996	1997	1998	1999	2000	Five-Year Total
	Capital						
	Hardware	663,000	5,963,000	9,937,000	6,625,000	4,969,000	28,157,000
	Applications and operating systems	215,000	1,535,000	2,476,000	1,650,000	1,238,000	7,114,000
	Telecommunications	94,000	846,000	1,410,000	940,000	705,000	3,995,000
	Interfaces	759,000	228,000	152,000	76,000	106,000	1,321,000
	Plant remodeling	28,000	254,000	423,000	282,000	212,000	1,199,000
	Peripheral equipment	59,000	531,000	885,000	590,000	442,000	2,507,000
	Sales tax	157,000	669,000	1,085,000	720,000	542,000	3,173,000
	Total capital	1,975,000	10,026,000	16,368,000	10,883,000	8,214,000	47,466,000

Operating							
	Telecommunications	2,000	37,000	191,000	412,000	561,000	1,203,000
	Staff	6,920,000	9,126,000	12,260,000	11,403,000	9,887,000	49,596,000
	Software and hardware maintenance	0	289,000	1,319,000	3,094,000	4,273,000	8,975,000
	Education and training	346,000	3,119,000	5,223,000	3,537,000	2,702,000	14,927,000
	Disaster avoidance/planning	12,000	108,000	180,000	120,000	90,000	510,000
	Total operating	7,280,000	12,679,000	19,173,000	18,566,000	17,513,000	75,211,000
Total Costs		9,255,000	22,705,000	35,541,000	29,449,000	25,727,000	122,677,000
Costs Less Benefits		$(8,605,000)	$(16,005,000)	$(17,684,000)	$(3,937,000)	$6,083,000	$(40,148,000)

- Capital and operating costs for the EMR/CDR are expected to be approximately $122,677,000 (including $47,466,000 in capital costs and $75,211,000 in operating costs). This includes costs for hardware, software, telecommunications, peripherals, and site modifications.
- Net costs (capital and operating costs net of expected benefits) are expected to be approximately $40,148,000 for the planning period. This is a forecast of actual benefits and costs over the planning period. Based on an implementation plan of five years, Sharp HealthCare would realize a positive return in year five.
- The annual EMR/CDR operating costs would reach 2.0 percent of the estimated 1996 total operating costs of $750 million.
- For the period from 1996 through 2000, Sharp projects approximately 9,777,000 outpatient encounters. Based on the projected net cost of $40,148,000 for the EMR/CDR, implementation of the new system would add approximately $4.10 to the cost of a visit.
- The current five-year EMR/CDR costs (approximately $40.1 million) have a net present value of approximately $35.8 million. This is based on application of a 6 percent annual discount rate (as used by Sharp HealthCare in its investment analysis) to projected future costs and benefits.

As noted in the ROI model, investments for staff training and for interfaces are expected to be approximately $16,248,000 over the planning period. These projects are currently under way, and funding is partially covered by other project budgets.

Table 4-3 summarizes the costs and benefits for Sharp HealthCare of implementing the EMR/CDR. Numbers are drawn from the feasibility model, and are rounded to the nearest thousand dollars. The assumptions in the ROI model related to the CDR are based on a design that provides long-term storage for clinical data and is the primary clinical decision support database. Assumptions related to the EMR are based on a design that employs client/server architecture with a graphical user interface. The EMR is used as the active patient clinical database for all on-line transaction processing (OLTP) environments. For estimated costs, the number of projected installed workstations was employed, rather than number of beds, hospitals, or encounters/admissions.

Information Systems Direction

Medical Service–Business Objectives Alignment

Sharp HealthCare is committed to using information technology that directly supports the larger organizational goals. Figure 4-4 illustrates the key Sharp business objectives driving IS requirements across the enterprise.

Realization of each of these goals requires enterprisewide integration of on-line clinical, demographic, and financial information regarding Sharp HealthCare patients and enrolled members. Implementation of the EMR/CDR is an essential component of this integration.

Figure 4-4. Major Sharp Goals Driving IS Requirements

Goal 1

Maintain/improve profitability

→

- Support comprehensive case management for entire continuum of care (e.g., home health, inpatient, clinical, and corporate services)
- Develop marketing database and reporting capability
- Support mobile work force through standard user interface, single-user log-on
- Enhance Sharp Foundation fund-raising capability

Goal 2

Maintain/enhance excellence in medical care and technical research and development

→

- Implement case management, outcomes assessment, clinical decision support, and prospective quality assurance
- Provide access to on-line patient history for entire continuum of care provided by Sharp HealthCare and its alliances
- Support Internet access and other on-line research
- Provide statistical analysis and on-demand proof of quality and outcomes measurements

Goal 3

Provide high-quality service on a regional basis; foster alliances with other key providers

→

- Enhance enterprisewide, high-bandwidth network usage, with connectivity to other potential partners
- Develop enterprisewide flexible reporting systems, allowing on-line data access
- Implement wide-area clinician access
- Access throughout provider community for the continuum of care

Goal 4

Redesign operations to enhance efficiency and productivity

→

- Exploit EDI
- Automate manual processes and complement process improvement
- Implement enterprisewide office automation, patient scheduling, data access, and report generation
- Integrate care elements for real-time access by multidisciplinary health care team

Goal 5

Position for success in managed care

→

- Extend enterprisewide managed care IS functionality
- Extend cost accounting and contract management systems to track costs and profits for cases and contracts
- Monitor and report patient/member satisfaction and wellness
- Facilitate information management for group contracting

User interviews conducted over the course of this project amplified the stated organizational goals. Not all organization goals are described here and some are summarized for the purposes of the EMR/CDR committee. Overall, cost identification, cost control, and associated functional reengineering remain prime management objectives.

Vision, Architecture, and Development Approach

Over the past five years, Sharp HealthCare has worked to acquire and evolve a common patient care information system. The primary objectives behind this strategy include:

- A single, organizationwide registration system
- Integrated on-line benefit eligibility
- Common clinical record with access throughout Sharp HealthCare
- The ability to support managed care contracting and utilization management
- Greater than 99 percent system availability

With the implementation of a patient-centered, enterprisewide EMR/CDR, Sharp HealthCare will advance its health information evolution, experience greater depth of information, and realize more comprehensive strategic reporting, as shown in figure 4-5.

There are 10 key issues facing Sharp HealthCare as it considers implementation of the EMR/CDR. The issues are especially relevant because of Sharp HealthCare's multientity structure and competitive marketplace. The committee considered these factors to be of such high importance that a plan to facilitate focus on these factors should begin immediately and be monitored continually. These 10 points, managed well, can significantly reduce the cost of implementation and maintenance of an EMR/CDR, as well as extend the intended benefits. Sharp HealthCare must:

- Develop staff members who can embrace and accept paradigm shifts in process
- Maintain an organization that learns, and is competent with change
- Focus on enterprisewide planning for design, selection, and implementation of new systems
- Manage process revisions by design
- Select systems and processes that minimize the time required to build and maintain user skill sets
- Design processes and systems that are characterized by ease of data capture and information retrieval
- Experience quick response time
- Develop and enforce data standards
- Provide system security and appropriate access
- Maintain and extend the enterprise master patient index

Figure 4-5. Sharp HealthCare Systems Vision for Integrated Health Care Information

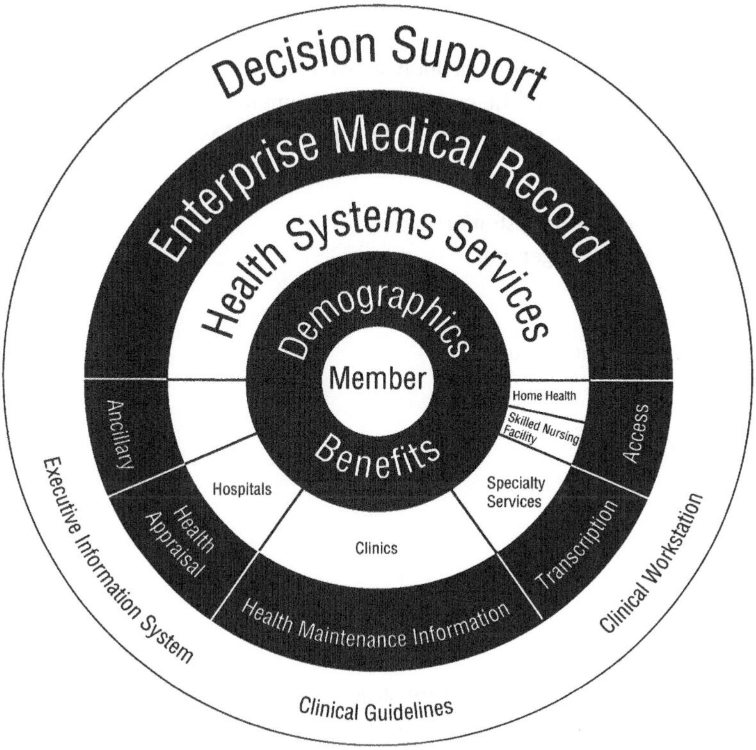

Application Requirements

From described user needs, 10 general technological requirements were identified. These requirements reflect the technology required to support users and to provide consistent, accurate documentation. They include:

1. Systems designed for capture of data at the point of care
2. Single-user sign-on access across application or system
3. Universal workstation access that would allow users to access the information with the same tools and similar instrumentation
4. Document scanning and retrieval
5. Imaging/picture archive computer systems
6. Integration of enterprise applications so that users may access pertinent information without switching from system to system

7. Interface engine technology that supports changes in requirements
8. "Open database" access to all data elements
9. Ability to query and perform database joins
10. Enterprisewide data repository

Specific requirements for application software, as identified through the requirements analysis, are detailed below. These requirements provide a core list of systems and functionalities required to fully support the EMR/CDR.

Administrative
- Master patient index/registration
- Encounter/ADT management
- Medical records
- Patient accounting
- Ambulatory patient tracking

Clinical
- Laboratory
- Radiology
- Pharmacy
- Surgery
- Cardiology
- Nurse staffing

Decision Support
- *Executive information system:* More structured and user-friendly than DSS, the EIS should include consolidated reporting and views of enterprise performance indicators, including trend analysis.
- Cost accounting
- Flexible budgeting
- Case management analysis
- Physician practice/protocol analysis
- Outcome measurements
- Referral pattern analysis
- Graphical data presentation

Electronic Medical Record/Clinical Data Repository
- On-line query
- Summary reporting
- Order entry
- Results reporting
- Scheduling
- Charting
- Clinical documentation
- Clinical case management

Financial
- General ledger
- Accounts payable
- Human resources
- Payroll
- Materials management

Telecommunications
- Electronic mail
- PC support tools

Managed Care
- Eligibility and enrollment
- Contract negotiation analysis
- Capitated referral management
- Reimbursement auditing and contract management
- Dues billing and accounting

Other Specialty/Extended Care
- Home health
- Skilled nursing

Physician Practice
- Physician billing/accounts receivable
- Contract management
- Scheduling
- Clinical protocols
- Practice promotion/marketing

Health Plan/Third-Party Administrative Systems
- Claims processing
- Enrollment
- Eligibility
- Authorization

Specific Strategies

There are a number of specific enabling substrategies that Sharp HealthCare can adopt to support the implementation and success of the EMR/CDR.

Network (Wide and Local Area)
- Create an enterprisewide system with universal terminal access to all applications
- Wide area network connecting all facilities with high bandwidth; capable of high-speed voice/data/image integration with minimal delays at peak volumes

- Ethernet network within each facility, with GUI interface
- Remote connections from all points of enterprise

Database
- Either standardize on one of the commercially available database products, or wait until one or more off-the-shelf applications are available to provide maximum bidding leverage.
- Add to vendor selection criteria that databases be relational in nature, if possible, one of the standard commercially available database products (for example, Oracle, Sybase, Ingres, Informix, RDB, DB2).

User Access
- Training must ensure that users are providing and receiving accurate, high-quality data, and that users have effective access to most of the information they require.
- Mechanics of using the system must be as straightforward and intuitive as possible.

Integration
- Move from current integration strategy (point-to-point interfaces with a limited number of vendors, and a core enterprise system) to interfaces via a hub technology/interface engine, with a limited number of vendors for the enterprise as a whole. This is the direction being used with the implementation of Cerner PathNet.

Community Health Information Network (CHIN)
- Consider at a later date a connection between Sharp HealthCare and a southern California or San Diego area CHIN. Through participation in such an organization, Sharp HealthCare could potentially:
  1. Provide a longitudinal, problem-oriented patient record that documents key events in the continuum of care across all facilities and entities, regardless of organizational affiliation
  2. Acquire and maintain demographic, financial, insurance, and encounter data
  3. Support referrals to Sharp HealthCare and provide links to affiliated, non-network health care providers
  4. Provide access to local, national, and regional medical network services to support review of medical literature, research, and recommended practice protocols

Workstation (Universal, Clinical, Administrative)
- End-user PCs and terminal
- Bedside/handheld devices for clinicians for point-of-care data capture
- Workstations for each end user, with high-speed and multimedia capability

Electronic Data Interchange
- Authorizations, claims, remittances
- Ultimate support of activities with associated providers, CHINs

PC Support Tools

- Expand electronic mail for enterprisewide communication
- Application support for word processing, electronic calendaring, committee management

Security and Data Integrity

- Fault-tolerant systems and networks engineered for zero downtime and full protection of data integrity
- System security with appropriate access, as determined by the Data Ownership and Access Policies

Data Ownership and Access Policies

Maintaining adequate security and integrity of Sharp HealthCare system data is of paramount importance throughout system planning, development, and maintenance efforts. Phase II of the EMR/CDR implementation plan provides for the development of network data standards. In developing these standards, Sharp HealthCare must clearly identify the composite user groups of information, together with the specific information they require to take full advantage of EMR/CDR capabilities. In this manner, Sharp HealthCare can determine the appropriate levels and types of access to network data.

Information Systems Benefits Projection

Strategic

Strategic benefits from the EMR/CDR are not typically directly quantifiable, but they have significant claim on Sharp's organizational direction and long-term viability. Benefits identified by the steering committee include:

- Increased market share
- Increased scope of service area
- Meet or beat competition regarding outcomes
- Position Sharp in selected areas as resource center with: increased prestige, increased MD recruitment, increased payer contracting, and increased research grant income
- Marketing and public service and image benefits due to high-quality advice, referral services
- Direct support of Sharp HealthCare business objectives
- Positions Sharp HealthCare as leading provider organization

Quantified

For the planning period 1996–2000, quantified benefits of the EMR/CDR implementation are projected to be approximately $82.5 million. This includes anticipated increases in revenues and membership, as well as decreases in operating costs due to the use of the EMR/CDR. In the ROI model, benefits have been phased in to reflect the phased implementation of the EMR/CDR.

Quantified benefits are based on:

- Increased membership and membership revenue, due to reduced membership turnover and increased market share
- Increased availability of medical records and other necessary information during physician visits
- Reduced nursing overtime costs
- Decreased courier and fax costs
- Decreased costs for medical records storage
- Decreased costs for chart abstracting and transcription
- Increased employee morale, with reduction in costs due to turnover and new employee recruitment; reduced training requirements
- Improved quality of care, with associated decreases in malpractice costs and costs of treating iatrogenic illness
- Improved cost-effectiveness of care, with more effective scheduling of resources and use of the continuum of care for Sharp HealthCare patients
- Improved patient education and preventive care
- Increased quality, completeness, integrity, and security of medical data

Of the benefits identified, roughly $45.8 million were specifically quantified. The remaining benefits were derived from estimates of revenue increases above the baseline (without EMR/CDR) of 0.125 percent per year, and costs being held to 2 percent per year below the projected baseline level. All revenue and cost projections include projected inflation of 3 percent per year.

Overall, numerous benefits are expected to accrue to each of the primary Sharp HealthCare EMR/CDR stakeholders, as illustrated below.

Benefits for Sharp HealthCare Patients

- Reduced delays and paperwork when registering for service, being admitted to the hospital, and scheduling appointments in advance
- Improved quality of care, due to timely, complete reporting of test results and avoidance of drug administration errors
- Reduced costs and separation from home and family, due to shorter hospital stays
- Reduced anxiety and delay while undergoing diagnosis and treatment, due to improved scheduling and due to faster reporting of results of tests and treatment
- Improved education in follow-up self-care, follow-up medical care, and wellness awareness

Benefits for Sharp HealthCare Physicians and Other Providers

- Improved access to information for patient care, due to access to the patient's medical record from anywhere in the enterprise

- More rapid, convenient provision of care, due to ability to update the patient's medical record at any time
- Improved quality of care, due to ability to review trends in the patient's condition on-line, for the current episode of care and over the long term
- Reduced risk of malpractice and adverse incidents, due to access to alerts and decision support to prevent complications and errors in diagnosis and treatment

Benefits for the Sharp HealthCare Enterprise and Administration

- Improved cost-effectiveness of care, due to on-line, longitudinal case management for the entire continuum of care
- Faster and more complete collection of revenue from third-party payers, due to automated abstracting and coding of diagnoses, procedures, and treatment plans, and capability for on-line submission of data
- Improved speed, convenience, and quality of compliance with JCAHO information management requirements and government reporting requirements (including record authentication)
- Improved administration of managed care populations, due to on-line verification of patient eligibility, benefits, and treatment authorization
- Improved contract administration and operation of managed care activity, due to contract modeling, outcomes analysis, and provider profile capability

ROI Analysis and Expectations

As noted in the return on investment model appended to this report, Sharp Health-Care must make a significant investment in order to install and realize full benefits from the EMR/CDR. After subtraction of projected benefits, the expected net cost to Sharp HealthCare for the EMR/CDR is approximately $40,148,000 over the five-year planning period.

Attainment Strategy and Guidelines

EMR/CDR Implementation

The prime goal is to optimize delivered functions while minimizing costs. Additional costs can be minimized by limiting the number of projects, vendors, interfaces, and end-user functions developed to those that can be managed by an experienced team. The ongoing information systems projects should still be managed by a core team of information management experts. This team can bring necessary resources together to accomplish the required goals. Additionally, to maintain user input and reference, an advisory team will be very helpful in supporting the implementation process.

Applications

Because so few ready-to-install applications are currently available, Sharp Health-Care may prefer to defer an immediate decision on an EMR application purchase.

Once vendors have accomplished several installations and the product functionality has been improved, Sharp HealthCare might find greater justification for implementation of an EMR. Greater functionality (applications) obtained from a single vendor is generally reflected in cost savings due to consistent end-user interfaces with the system, which relates directly to the amount of time needed to train staff. This issue carries forward for the entire duration that the software is installed, due to recurring upgrades requested by Sharp HealthCare, or by a new release of software provided by the vendor. Each successive upgrade could require end-user training that is directly related to high costs and implementation delays. Staff size plays a big role in the total training cost—8,000 staff and 2,000 physicians need training.

Vendor

Because the partnership initiated with the vendor(s) must be close and profitable for both organizations, selecting a stable vendor with vision and product will be the best approach. This vendor must embrace the same critical success factors as Sharp HealthCare. This vendor will also be capable of demonstrating that it can adapt to changing business and clinical needs. Finally, the vendor must be able to accommodate changing business directions over the life of the software. Until Sharp HealthCare has several options available to them in, at least, a beta version, Sharp HealthCare may choose to defer any decision.

Project Management

The number of different projects and/or different vendors will have an exponential influence on project cost. Initial cost projections indicate that the first three years of the project need the strongest commitment for project administration to establish strong development and implementation methodologies. It is best not to have the contracted firms responsible for project management. Instead, Sharp HealthCare should consider the use of its own staff for the management, design, and building of the EMR/CDR. An appropriate mix of vendor, consulting, and user representation on the team will provide significant value.

Note

1. Any endeavor of this size requires a tremendous effort and commitment from participants. Unfortunately, the Sharp HealthCare and JDA staff who offered invaluable contributions to the project's success are too numerous to be acknowledged individually, although a number of professionals, including Edward Kopetsky, then senior VP/CIO of Sharp HealthCare; Sandra McCullough, RN, EMR/CDR Committee chair; and Thomas Mack, RPh, JDA project supervisor, need to be recognized for having been instrumental in starting and driving the Sharp initiative.

Leadership for Achieving Breakthrough Benefits

Taking full advantage of information technology (IT) potential requires a multifaceted approach to examining, evaluating, and implementing systems and technologies. Numerous planning and management tools exist to aid executive decision makers in mastering this approach. In the end, however, to a large extent success depends on the talents and abilities of executive leadership. Those executives able to develop a wholistic approach to IT investment will bring the greatest benefits, both incremental and breakthrough, to their organizations. Such a skill must be developed over time, through iterative investment reward and return cycles.

Planning and achieving incremental benefits should be a routine aspect of IT management. Achieving success in more complicated breakthrough initiatives requires an organizational and managerial commitment of a greater magnitude and intensity. However, the potential for such path-breaking gains in efficiency and effectiveness does exist both within and across organizations. This chapter ties together the concepts illustrated throughout this book, with particular focus on the ongoing nature and characteristics of breakthrough strategies and benefits. Specific discussion topics include:

- A review of the basic concepts and characteristics behind breakthrough investing
- Key steps in facilitating the achievement of breakthrough benefits
- Cautions to consider when planning, reviewing, or initiating a potential breakthrough investment

Reviewing the Breakthrough Concept

Strategies designed to achieve breakthrough benefits share a number of characteristics relating to the intensity, duration, and cost magnitude of the effort required to execute the strategy. Breakthrough benefits include hard economic, clinical, or psychological elements, but are characterized by the difficulty in fully quantifying their effects. Although potential returns may be large, direct measurement and attribution may be difficult. The key characteristics of breakthrough strategies include:

- They involve *significant change* in the way organizations do business. Internal relationships (for example, administrators and physicians) as well as external relationships (for example, providers and payers, providers and patients) change. Breakthrough strategies involve designing — engineering, if you will — new ways to accomplish new activities that incorporate old tasks. For example, some capitated managed care plans now offer members a point-of-service option, where they can choose to exit the capitated network according to certain requirements and financial restrictions. To the provider, this necessitates a mechanism to approve and track this "point-of-service exiting," through cutting referral letters, notifying appropriate plan officials, and monitoring contract payments, with activities beginning immediately upon seeing the patient.
- Breakthrough strategies require *longer economic return cycles,* running in the 3 to 10 year range, as opposed to incremental benefits, which may be realized in 18 months or less.
- *Implementation costs are higher,* comparatively, than for projects offering incremental gains in cost or efficiency. Generally, financing is done through the *capital budget* rather than the operating budget.
- *Enthusiastic sponsorship* of the new strategy is essential at the top of the organization, including boards, administrators, physicians, and community stakeholders.
- *Risks are substantial.* Although preventive measures can reduce risk, a high degree of organizational exposure to various kinds of risk is unavoidable. Most breakthrough strategies involve at least targeted use of emerging (unproven) technologies, carrying higher risk to the organization. The level of organizational change inherent in a breakthrough strategy also carries a level of risk; managing that change must be a distinct component of the overall breakthrough strategy.

As health care remains poised at the brink of fundamental change, cost-cutting and service control measures can accomplish only so much. A number of currently popular techniques, including business process reengineering, reflect an industry acceptance that examination of business and medical management processes is necessary to ensure ongoing survival and success. Such techniques, although they support the achievement of breakthrough benefits, also can fall short. With the scope and magnitude of change facing health care, in some cases, processes and procedures are required to support a completely new business model — nothing exists to reengineer. To progress beyond that point, providers must examine and revise the fundamental ways they do business, engineering an approach to success.

Formation of a new business and medical service model is one of the most persuasive reasons for providers to adopt breakthrough IT strategies. Other motivations typically cited by organizations include a mix of economic and quality concerns, and strategic positioning for market share and/or the capture of managed care contracts and covered lives.

Achieving Breakthrough Momentum

The imperatives driving change in health care will not subside. Pressure to improve the cost-effectiveness of and access to care, the ongoing growth of managed care capitation, state efforts at health care reform, ongoing legal and regulatory requirements on providers, and continuing evidence of the importance of population health status are only some of the forces supporting change and evolution in the U.S. industry.

The new and changing financial, clinical, and administrative information requirements associated with these imperatives have far-reaching implications on IT development and use. In answer to these requirements, technology is moving in two distinct directions:

1. *Technology in support of community and population health status, with a comprehensive, continuum of care view, is growing rapidly.* The health care continuum is moving quickly to support more than just the delivery of care. All aspects of the industry—financing, wellness, acute intervention, prevention—are moving toward an integrated model. Some of the implications for technology include:
   - Increased emphasis on patient risk assessment, education, risk reduction, and lifestyle modification
   - Development of effective longitudinal case management approaches
   - Growing importance of the public health function—tracking population health status
   - Increased emphasis on access and manipulation of clinical, financial, and population risk data by larger numbers of stakeholders
2. *Technological applications in clinical informatics are expanding tremendously, including the electronic medical and health record.* As development of clinical technologies continues its rapid pace, some of the implications for technology include:
   - Growth of clinical data repositories, supporting actuarial and outcomes research on a longitudinal basis
   - Increased availability of diagnostic, procedure, and protocol support
   - Increased direct-technology use by physicians and other care providers
   - Growing requirements for integrating the clinical, financial, and quality sides of care

There are a number of steps that provider organizations can take to develop an environment conducive to breakthrough thinking. Although no single one will ensure success, each offers a building block toward optimal IT planning and use.

Build a core competency in the use of information technology. Evolve that competency to a distinct one that differentiates the organization from others in the market. Integrating IT planning and execution into the larger organizational scheme will serve to both secure incremental benefits and build an enterprisewide atmosphere of trust in information technology and IT staff. This supportive relationship is critical to the success of any breakthrough project.

In addition, advanced IT projects and strategies rely on the support of a core IT infrastructure (technology, staff, and savvy users). For example, the electronic medical record (EMR) project discussed in chapter 4 is dependent on the effective design and implementation of an enterprisewide area network. Without such a network, access to the EMR is inhibited and breakthrough benefits will not be obtained. In addition, the project is dependent on increasing the information systems (IS) skill level of end users such that sophisticated systems can become part of their everyday work experience.

Evaluate carefully whether the need is for redesign, reengineering, or new design. Organizations should clearly identify information requirements and measure existing IT capabilities against those requirements. If the two do not match, it is critical to identify the causes. These may include changes in organizational structure (for example, merger, affiliation), market shifts (such as with growth in managed care), outdated investments, suboptimal implementation of current IT capabilities, or a new business mission.

Concentrate first on small wins. Particularly when using emerging technologies, small-scale, pilot implementation and proof of concept can prove effective in minimizing risk and optimizing benefits. One provider organization, interested in the potential of handheld technology, began by investing in equipment for the labor and delivery areas. Staff used handhelds to log births and generate birth certificates. By investing on this scale, the organization was able to document the full-time equivalent (FTE) time savings achieved through the technology, celebrate this success, and plan for effective wide-scale implementation.

Build from and accumulate success. Projects should be planned so that each small success positions the organization to achieve the next. As IT staff and users see the demonstrable results of each small investment, the larger goal being pursued becomes defined and achievable. When a major effort, breakthrough, or large incremental project is required, the organization will have the confidence, based on small gains, to move forward to larger challenges.

Commit to a consistent, ongoing education and training effort. An ongoing executive commitment to IT education and training—for end users, senior management, and IS staff—can greatly increase the value and benefits of IT investments. The benefits of existing systems and technologies are optimized by knowledgeable personnel; additionally, by making education and training an ongoing and consistent effort, organization perception of the value of information systems/technology rises. A perpetual, continuous benefits maximization effort results. This increased awareness of IT worth is invaluable when trying to generate support and buy-in for new or complicated technology projects.

Plan, monitor, evaluate, replan, and correct. The clearest way to develop a distinct competency in IS technology is through a continual learning process—and practice. If the initial plan for an investment fails to perform as anticipated, the course of that investment must be corrected through scope changes, incremental reinvestments, or, in worst-case scenarios, discontinuing or replacing the technology. This iterative process will not only ensure that the performance of organizational dollars is monitored on an ongoing basis, but it also may well open opportunities that were unanticipated at the onset of the investment.

Balance the flow of costs and benefits. Beware of projects promising great benefits downstream, with large upfront capital and operational requirements. Any investment will require an initial outlay, but there should be some parity between financial expenditures and benefits. If, during implementation of a technology, benefits do not begin to appear as anticipated, the provider organization must identify why. Some potential causes for misalignment between costs and benefits include: benefits were overstated during planning; costs were understated; or plan activities have not been implemented aggressively enough.

Be conscious of industry trends affecting organizational revenue flow. Current industry trends, particularly managed care and capitation, have the potential to change or reduce the flow of money to the provider organization on short notice. Movement to a more fixed-cost structure can create margin pressure on organizations, affecting the capital allocation process. IT capital requests must compete not only against routine replacement and maintenance projects, but also against urgent strategic initiatives such as physician practice acquisitions.

Watch for hidden precedent costs. To be fully effective, some technologies require that a core technological infrastructure be in place and operational. Sometimes provider organizations understate precedent costs for a technology, particularly those related to telecommunications, training, or related infrastructure requirements. These costs may be buried in other projects and budgets. For example, an organization using clinical data repository (CDR) technology cannot receive the full benefits of the CDR unless all enterprise information can be incorporated into the repository. A certain level of networking, data communications, and data standards technology must be employed.

Incorporate return-on-investment (ROI) analysis into routine IT management. ROI analysis should be built into systems and technology planning. Whether an organization chooses to build systems from the ground up or to purchase applications from IT vendors, benefits return should automatically be a critical consideration.

Consciously evaluate the level of ROI analysis required. It is unlikely that an organization will have the time and resources to microanalyze ROI for every potential IT investment. On a case-by-case basis, the ROI decision should be made according to investment size and complexity, level of change likely required to implement the investment, and executive comfort. The analysis technique and level of detail should be structured based on these factors, without overanalyzing projects that do not require tremendous specificity.

Work with technology vendors. Provider organizations are not in the business of manufacturing technology solutions. Often they never reach the true capacity of current systems and future technologies. However, there are strategies in dealing with technology and systems vendors that can increase the utility and effectiveness of technology investments. Key among these is a provider commitment to aggressive account management and planning structure. Clear and continuing communication between provider and technology or HIS vendor is the best possible way to optimize investment dollars.

In some cases, provider organizations may find the potential benefits of a development relationship to be worth the inherent risk involved (as discussed in chapter 1). Risk- and reward-sharing relationships, if carefully considered, can result in high rewards for both organizations.

Assessing the Health Care Landscape

Getting the most out of information technology will not happen overnight. By laying a foundation for reasonable and prudent IT investments, however, organizations can avoid being blindly swept along with the requirements of a rapidly evolving market. With a concerted effort, the same organizations can simultaneously achieve consistent IT benefits, transform to a new business/medical service model, and evolve to a central management core competency.

Actively work to articulate a fundamental IT vision that is harmonious to the mission and vision of your larger organization. Dedicate yourself to a new investment vision. Plan your course, follow and correct, but enjoy the journey.

IT Features, Functionalities, and Projected Benefits

As discussed in chapter 2, the particular features and functionalities of an information system (IS) drive the benefits an organization might expect from its implementation and use. In these tables, features and functionalities are correlated to those expected benefits. Benefits are meant to illustrate both the strategic and the incremental gains possible through use of a particular technology.

This appendix is organized similarly to chapter 2—networking and telecommunications and electronic data interchange (EDI) tables precede the actual application software tables, which include:

- Networking and telecommunications
- Electronic data interchange
- General financial systems
- Patient financial and administrative systems
- Decision support systems
- Provider managed care systems
- Payer managed care systems
- Clinical systems
- Home health systems
- Ancillary department systems

Benefits found from the use of networking, telecommunication, or EDI technologies in conjunction with a specific application software are listed in the earlier tables, rather than the specific software listing.

One caveat: Reflecting the whole range and functionality of today's information systems is a difficult task to undertake. The tables in this section, rather than a comprehensive listing, are intended to illustrate the connection between features and functionalities. The speed of technological development and innovation requires an assumption that new features, benefits, and functionalities will have emerged by the time this information is published.

Networking and Telecommunications

Problem to Be Addressed	Technology Feature/Functionality	Projected Benefits	Benefit Measurement Criteria
Accounts Receivable			
Delayed or incomplete patient bills, from departmental/service coordination problems	• Automated charge capture from ancillary services posts directly to patient accounts • Order-entry interface or integration captures charges and services as they occur	Real-time charge capture allows faster billing, even possibly as patient completes care episode or services	Amount of time to prepare patient bills; postage costs; accounts/receivable (A/R) days; recouped charge revenue
Lost patient charges	Links between clinical/ancillary systems and patient financials allow direct input of patient charges	Increased charge capture	$ value of captured charges
Manual data collection and entry for claims submission requires large FTE resource commitment	Links between billing and claims databases allow data transfer	Reduced or eliminated manual data entry; faster claims compilation and submission	FTE time commitment required for claims; # of days between patient service and claims submission
Admission, Discharge, Transfer (ADT)			
Multiple points of registration require redundant data collection	• Enterprise access to master patient index (MPI) • Single ADT system accessible from throughout the facility	Less redundancy in data collection; increased accuracy; better tracking of patient groups and utilization across the enterprise	# of redundant patient records; time spent conducting ADT activities
Interface Engines			
Department/facility staff unable to agree on single or compatible information systems supplier(s)	Interface engine allows connection of different/incompatible systems	Freedom to select systems for performance, rather than compatibility; improved user satisfaction	User satisfaction
Information transfer across departments/ facilities slow, paper oriented, and prone to error/delay	• Interface engine connects systems requiring common data • Data transfer across systems requires little human intervention	Reduced paper transfer; fewer delays, errors	Information collection/research time required for administrative, patient care activities
Local/Wide Area Networks			
Delays or difficulties in adding new facilities, users to IS backbone	Standard hardware, software, protocols	Faster integration of new facilities and users	FTE time spent in bringing new facilities, users up on enterprise network, systems
Delays in obtaining information; heavy volume of internal phone traffic; staff time spent tracking necessary information	Facility or enterprisewide e-mail	Faster, more efficient communication across departments, facilities	Volume of internal calls; volume of e-mail packets sent and received

Networking and Telecommunications (Continued)

Problem to Be Addressed	Technology Feature/Functionality	Projected Benefits	Benefit Measurement Criteria
Local/Wide Area Networks (Continued)			
Employees required to move across departments, facilities find it difficult to use and access unfamiliar systems, machines	Standard hardware, software, protocols	Easier for employees to move between physical locations; increased user satisfaction; reduced training required for such transfers	Amount of training required for transfers; user satisfaction of transferred employees
Inconsistent versions of software throughout facility require maintenance, training	Centralized, standard versions of software accessible throughout facility	More efficient licensing and compliance with copyright regulations; standard software simplifies user training; centralized maintenance contracting reduces cost, internal resource requirements	# of software contracts; # of different software versions and programs in use; cost (if in existence) of formal user training programs; FTE staff time required to maintain multiple software applications
Multiple hardware platforms in use throughout facility require maintenance, training	Standard hardware, protocols	More efficient licensing and maintenance contracting; standard protocols simplify user training; reduced complexities	#, cost of hardware maintenance contracts; # of different hardware platforms, protocols in use; FTE staff time required to maintain multiple platforms
Materials Management			
Expensive medical equipment is misplaced or lost	Infrared location badges indicate location of equipment within facility	Reduction in number of lost or misplaced items; better tracking of facility capital investments; staff spends less time searching for misplaced equipment	# of misplaced or lost pieces of equipment; time spent in locating equipment
High on-hand inventory value	Links with other hospital systems, electronically tracks inventory requested versus used	Reduced requirements for on-hand inventory, funds previously dedicated to materials can be diverted to other areas	$ value of inventory maintained by facility
On-hand inventory requires large, dedicated facility space	Electronic tracking of required levels of inventory	Reduced requirements for on-hand inventory frees facility space for other purposes	Amount of inventory space required, $ value of freed facility space
Medical Records			
Delays in patient scheduling, processing due to physician need to access and review information	Caregivers can remotely access medical record, scheduling information	Improved patient satisfaction through fewer delays in care; staff time savings for locating and obtaining information	# of patients preregistered or preadmitted from remote locations; FTE time dedicated to information-gathering activities

(Continued on next page)

Networking and Telecommunications (Continued)

Problem to Be Addressed	Technology Feature/Functionality	Projected Benefits	Benefit Measurement Criteria
Medical Records (Continued)			
High facsimile and courier costs to ensure flow of information to remote physicians, enterprise locations	Caregivers can remotely access medical record, scheduling information	Reduced need for facsimile, courier transmissions; time savings for FTE to prepare and send transmissions	# of packages sent by fax or courier; cost of fax network, courier services; paper savings (cost, storage)
Telecommunications			
Collection staff unable to keep pace with work volume	Predictive dialer: • Automatically dials phone number • Downloads and displays patient account information when phone is answered	Increased productivity	Volume of collections calls by staff FTE; reduced receivables; reduced "bad debt" write-offs
High long-distance telephone charges	"Smart" router automatically selects lowest-cost long-distance line	Reduced phone charges	$ spent on telephone long-distance charges
Inpatient and outpatient registration time-consuming, often delays care	Telephone registration system allows preregistration of inpatient and outpatient groups	Less delay for incoming patients, improved patient satisfaction with care experience, more complete information collected	Time spent by patients in on-site registration; patient satisfaction; # of incomplete patient registrations
Large resource commitment required to process heavy volume of patient calls	• Automated call processor directs callers to appropriate department • Automated information tapes provide commonly requested information (i.e., pretest regimens, basic health information)	Fewer misdirected calls; increased patient satisfaction; reduced FTE time requirement to process call volume; increased productivity of existing FTEs; improved patient and community satisfaction	# of misdirected/incomplete calls; patient/community satisfaction; FTE time requirement to process call volume; # of calls processed
Noise from paging and intercom systems negatively affecting inpatient satisfaction	• Wireless voice call communications system offers unit paging functionality • One-way communications paging system noiselessly communicates basic messages to staff	Decrease in number of pages, intercoms; reduced noise problems; increased patient satisfaction	# of unit pages; patient satisfaction

Electronic Data Interchange

Problem to Be Addressed	Technology Feature/Functionality	Projected Benefits	Benefit Measurement Criteria
Eligibility, Claims, Accounts Receivable (A/R)			
Delays or long lead times in claims A/R; resource-intensive claims follow-up	• Claims electronically submitted to payers • Electronic remittance of claims payments • System users electronically notified when claims are incomplete/rejected	Reduced A/R; reduced A/R days; electronic submission speeds claims process; electronic alerts make users aware of problems in a more timely fashion	A/R days; total A/R
High postal, forms, telephone costs to submit and monitor outstanding claims; or high mail/courier charges from providing payers with follow-up information to document care	• Electronic submission of claims • Status of pending claims can be verified on-line • Electronic links to payers	Reduced forms, courier, postage requirements; reduced necessary telephone follow-up of pending claims; improvement in staff productivity through elimination of manual tracking systems	$ spent on forms, postage, courier, telephone costs; FTE time spent tracking pending claims
Large FTE time commitment for claims activities	• Electronic submission of claims • Status of pending claims can be verified on-line • On-line eligibility • Electronic notification of incomplete/rejected claims, including explanation	Automation of submission, claims monitoring reduces FTE time commitment required for claims-related activities; FTE productivity increases	Amount of FTE time required in claims activities; volume of claims processed per FTE
Large FTE time commitment to verify patient eligibility	Provider staff can verify patient eligibility in an on-line transaction	Staff spends less time tracking patient eligibility; possible reduction in care delays; eliminates bulky payer-supplied enrollment/eligibility lists	FTE time spent in eligibility verification activities; # of times care is delayed because of missing/unavailable eligibility information
Lost revenue through inability/difficulty in coordination of benefits between multiple payers	EDI capabilities allow for automatic tracking of coordination of benefits (COB) limits and submission requirements	Better coordination of benefits increases revenue capture	Revenue captured through payer claims
Unpredictable cash flow from claims A/R	Electronic submission and monitoring of pending claims	Stable, predictable flow of cash from submitted claims	Days to payment on submitted claims
Unpredictable cash flow from fee for service (FFS) A/R	Electronic funds transfer allows patients to debit bills directly from banking accounts	Improved cash flow; reduced follow-up on accounts; more predictable approximation of facility receivables	# of accounts assigned to collections; A/R days from FFS patient groups
Materials Management			
High cost of facility purchase orders	Electronic submission and confirmation of orders through standard interface	Reduced cost for materials orders	Per purchase order cost

(Continued on next page)

Electronic Data Interchange (Continued)

Problem to Be Addressed	Technology Feature/Functionality	Projected Benefits	Benefit Measurement Criteria
Materials Management (Continued)			
High costs of inventory supplies, materials	• Large-scale contracting and electronic orders capability • Electronic comparison of ordered goods, pricing to ensure contract compliance	Streamlined ordering reduces costs; contract compliance capabilities ensure accurate charges	Per purchase order cost; contracted = actual materials costs
Supply cost, number of suppliers increase costs, staff requirements	EDI capabilities with standard suppliers allows: • Electronic supply-ordering capability • Real-time verification that order is received, in stock at supplier	Fewer required paper transactions, lower paper costs; negotiated (discounted) supply rates; more efficient ordering reduces on-hand inventory	# of paper orders; amount of space required for on-hand inventory; supply costs; paper costs; cost per purchase order

General Financial Systems

Problem to Be Addressed	Technology Feature/Functionality	Projected Benefits	Benefit Measurement Criteria
Accounts Payable (A/P), Payroll			
Decentralized A/P leads to redundant efforts, multiple contracts	System can maintain A/P for multiple facilities, business units, discrete functions (i.e., patient refunds)	Consolidated contracting allows organization to optimize terms, reducing costs; saved staff time increases productivity, reduces FTEs	# of duplicate contracts; A/P costs; # of A/P FTE; A/P FTE productivity levels
Heavy staff resource requirements for A/P and financial functions	Automated financial management capabilities. Tape and automated routines might include: • Purchase order (PO) generation • 1099 reporting • Check reconciliation • Remittance reporting	More efficient financial management, fewer required staff resources	# of FTEs
High administrative overhead in producing and maintaining payroll-related data	• System allows flexible earnings and deductions coding, with batch and interactive data-entry capabilities • Prepares state and federal reports and tapes • Includes salary planning, budget versus actual and other FTE-related activities • Supports multiple facilities and divisions	Automation of procedures reduces required FTEs, paperwork in this function	Payroll FTEs; paper costs
Fixed Assets			
Poor tracking and control of enterprise fixed assets	• Maintains records of capital purchases • Calculates monthly depreciation • Inventory of items by physical class, maintenance information, and inventory tags	Clearly identified assets; automated depreciation optimizes financial value of assets with minimal financial staff intervention	Accurate fixed-assets data for reporting and analysis purposes
Materials Management			
Decentralized inventories create redundancy in effort, stock	Central materials management system tracks multiple inventory locations	Better monitoring of enterprisewide inventory reduces redundant orders.	Supply costs
Inventory maintenance and ordering requires large staff resource commitment	System automates laborious manual tasks, including: • Tracks stock levels • Automatically generates required POs (based on actual or scheduled use) • Reconciles invoices and received supplies • Transfers appropriate information to fixed-asset system	Reduced staff requirements for inventory control; lower costs per PO	Department productivity levels; # of required FTEs; per PO cost

(Continued on next page)

General Financial Systems (Continued)

Problem to Be Addressed	Technology Feature/Functionality	Projected Benefits	Benefit Measurement Criteria
Materials Management (Continued)			
Large on-hand inventory demands large physical space commitment	• Functionalities supporting "just-in-time" purchasing • Inventory tracking notes low levels of stock, generates alert	Freed space for income-generating activities; cost savings from satellite rentals; more efficient distribution of inventory costs	Amount of required physical space for inventory; reduced annual inventory costs
Lost revenue from uncaptured chargeable use of materials	• Central system assigns supply use for chargeable materials (i.e., through bar coding) • System interface feeds charges to patient accounting	Better capture of patient charges for supplies	Revenue from patient inventory charges; % of charges for supplies lost

Patient Financial and Administrative Systems

Problem to Be Addressed	Technology Feature/Functionality	Projected Benefits	Benefit Measurement Criteria
Accounts Receivable (A/R), Collections			
Account collection follow-up activities require large FTE commitment	• Claim tracking generates automated billing worklists • Allows user-specified criteria for automatic transfer to bad debt • Prepares collection letter based on user-defined criteria • Allows ability to conduct in-house collection activities prior to turnover to collection agency • Automatically transfers unpaid selected third-party balances to self-pay status after facility-defined period of time • Automated follow-up notices based on user-defined criteria (i.e., patient type, financial class)	Automated activities save FTE time, facilitate consistent follow-up on A/R	A/R days; $ bad debt; FTE A/R/collections staff
Disproportionately high A/R FTE labor overhead costs; or A/R FTE staff unable to process A/R patient volume	• Electronic payment posting • Automatic adjustments and write-offs • Electronic bill edits	Reduced FTE time commitment; increased staff productivity	$ A/R FTE; A/R FTE process volume
Facility has difficulty generating accurate patient billings in a timely fashion, affecting overall facility days in A/R; and/or a high volume of claims are returned/rejected, not paid	• Order-entry system generates charges at time of order or service provision • System generates billing forms, according to payer specifications • User-defined bill holds, or warning for incomplete billing information • Provides on-line and batch entry of charges and adjustments • System maintains multiple price structures on each line item for different payers and patient types • Automatic adjustment for user-specified discounts • User-defined billing cycles (i.e., interim, discharge, demand and rebilling) • Electronic claims processing and payment posting to/from payers	Faster, more accurate bill preparation speeds time to billing, decreases overall A/R; decreases # of payer rebills required; reduces lost charges	Time to billing; A/R days; # of bills returned because of errors, incorrect formats
High A/R days due to difficulty in addressing and delivering patient bills	• System verifies that address input in patient administration system is deliverable • System automatically generates bills with postal standard addresses (i.e., CA, rather than CA. or Cal.) • System sorts, bar-codes, and bundles bills to qualify for postal discounts	Reduction in amount of mail returned as undeliverable; postage cost savings from fewer returned pieces, postal discounts; time savings from less required follow-up of returned bills; reduced A/R days	# of pieces of mail returned as undeliverable; postage costs; FTEs required for postal follow-up; average days in A/R

(Continued on next page)

Patient Financial and Administrative Systems (Continued)

Problem to Be Addressed	Technology Feature/Functionality	Projected Benefits	Benefit Measurement Criteria
Accounts Receivable (A/R), Collections (Continued)			
Inaccurate A/R costing facility revenue	• Payments automatically posted to correct accounts • Calculations automatically balance • Consistent bill edit checks • Single point of data entry	Reduced/eliminated redundant data collection saves time, lowers potential for human error; more accurate A/R	$ A/R revenue
Admission/Registration, Discharge and Transfer, Master Patient Index			
Data lost in patient transfers (bed, input to output, output to input, real transfers and data corrections) results in redundant data collection, lost charges	• Database for use in charging and billing for services • When patient transferred, generates printout of all necessary information for area receiving patient • Automated transfer of all patient information and/or revenue reclassification, statistical updates when patient is transferred • User-defined requirements and designation, correction, or actual transfer	Outpatient registration allows status transfers (e.g., emergency to inpatient), reducing confusion, capturing uncharged items	FTE time required to process transfers; $ revenue from charges
Delays in care due to missing, incomplete data required by facility administrative, clinical staff	• Preregistration capabilities allow data collection to begin before patients present for care • System generates medical records "pull slips" • System generates preregistration reports with information requirements highlighted	Staff able to proactively track information needs for scheduled patients; improved patient satisfaction through better preparation by medical facility staff	# of care delays due to missing, incomplete information; patient satisfaction with service
Delays and errors in outpatient visit registrations	• Electronic access to prior history and visit information • Provides for decentralized registration capability (e.g., registration by radiology staff for radiology outpatients) • Online registration for same-day surgery patients • Eliminates need for reregistration of returning patients by maintaining patient information history file • Automatically generates electronic log for each outpatient area	Outpatient registration speeds process and ensures greater accuracy	Average time per ADT event; # of errors in ADT events
Facility has difficulty tracking and identifying characteristics of patient population	• On-line review of MPI to access/review previous patient stay information • Ad hoc reporting capabilities for collected data (such as LOS by diagnosis, MTD and YTD census)	Automated ADT provides greater marketing outreach through use of prior information and preadmission capabilities; collects and	Availability of patient population and use statistics

Patient Financial and Administrative Systems (Continued)

Problem to Be Addressed	Technology Feature/Functionality	Projected Benefits	Benefit Measurement Criteria
Admission/Registration, Discharge and Transfer, Master Patient Index (Continued)			
	• Data collection, storage, and retrieval of user-required patient information • Census statistics information • Captures referring physician name and phone number • User-defined admission/registration screens allow facility to customize data capture • Ad hoc reporting, such as LOS by diagnosis, MTD and YTD census • Displays patients by physician or physician group	stores essential patient origin, physician referral, and related statistics for further research and analysis	
Large FTE commitment required to process patient through admission, discharge, transfer activities; difficulties in completing ADT processes in an accurate and timely fashion	• MPI access at all points of admission/registration • Automatically interfaces with card writer and ID bracelet embosser • Generates appropriate admission forms and labels • ADT notices for appropriate departments; patient transfers generate printout/on-line notification of all necessary information for area receiving patient • Assigns new medical record and financial numbers when appropriate; allows for confidential and special patient designations • Automatically generates discharge instructions • System supports "hot key" shortcuts (i.e., zip code entry automatically provides city and state) • Ability to update diagnosis prior to discharge • On-line inquiry to verify that all outstanding items have been cleared at discharge	Automated ADT eliminates significant paperwork, forms, labels, and card preparation, reducing FTE requirements and increasing patient satisfaction; redundant data collection is reduced and human points of potential failure are minimized	FTEs required for ADT activities; average time per ADT event
Large FTE commitment to process outpatient populations through registration, discharge and transfer activities	• Electronic access to prior history and visit information • On-line registration for same-day surgery patients • Eliminates need for reregistration of returning patients by maintaining patient information history file • Generates appropriate registration forms and labels	Outpatient registration decreases repetitive paperwork and registration time through access to prior-visit information	FTE required for ADT activities; average time per ADT event

(Continued on next page)

Patient Financial and Administrative Systems (Continued)

Problem to Be Addressed	Technology Feature/Functionality	Projected Benefits	Benefit Measurement Criteria
Admission/Registration, Discharge and Transfer, Master Patient Index (Continued)			
	• MPI access at time of registration • User-defined registration screens allow facility customization of data collection • System supports "hot key" shortcuts (i.e., zip code entry automatically provides city and state)		
Multiple points of admission/registration generate redundant data gathering and entry, • Increasing staff FTE time commitment • Negatively affecting patient satisfaction	• Access from all locales to enterprise MPI • Access to prior-visit/history information • Preregistration capabilities allow data collection before patient presents for care	Reduces/eliminates redundant data capture; reduces FTE commitment; reduces length of patient wait at admission/registration improves patient satisfaction	Time spent in admissions/registration; patient satisfaction
Bed Control, Census			
Incorrect or uncaptured bed charges decreasing hospital revenue	• Allows maintenance of multiple room rates for each bed • Accurate tracking of transfers, discharges • Electronic/automated capture of room charge for billing	Patients are billed correctly by bed type; automatic data capture ensures hospital receives deserved moneys	$ revenue from bed charges; # of errors in patient billings
Large FTE time requirement in tracking and updating bed status information; admitting physicians cannot easily obtain bed availability or patient census information	• Maintains on-line census • Supports electronic inquiry to determine bed status (e.g., empty and ready, empty not ready) • Automatic update of patient census as bed assignment and bed changes are made • Census inquiry by parameters such as medical service, attending physician	Reduced clerical and time requirements in accessing bed control information; real-time data access monitors patient census and bed availability data	FTEs required for bed control activities; amount of time required for admitting physicians to access required data
LOS calculations time-consuming or often in error because of manual processes (statistical errors)	• Maintains on-line census • Automatically calculates patient LOS	More accurate, less FTE time commitment; clearer understanding of facility utilization assists management in contract negotiations	# of LOS errors

Patient Financial and Administrative Systems (Continued)

Problem to Be Addressed	Technology Feature/Functionality	Projected Benefits	Benefit Measurement Criteria
Medical Records			
Difficulty in accessing medical record information in a timely fashion	Optical storage of medical information	Improved speed and access to information needed by caregivers; associated improvement in timeliness and quality of care; simplifies retrieval, reducing FTE time requirements and retrieval costs	Patient LOS; # of unnecessary procedures; # of ADEs; average retrieval time for information requests
High costs for maintaining required medical or financial records	Optical storage of information	Reduction/elimination of paper/microfilm records, with associated space, paper, folder, and microfilm savings	Value of space saved, paper/microfilm costs versus cost of storage technology
Incomplete/deficient charts delaying billing	• Chart deficiency analyses by category, physician, and age of deficiency • Automatic alerts of deficiencies and their associated billing/reimbursement delay implications • Automatic bill holds based on degree of chart completion and third-party payer requirements	More efficient tracking of deficiencies eliminates "overlooks," speeds billing; report capabilities identify recurrent offenders (type of deficiency and physician) indicating need for corrective strategy	# of deficient charts; FTE follow-up required for chart completion; A/R days
Incomplete medical records, high required follow-up by medical records (MR) staff after patient departure; delayed reimbursement	• Electronic alerts sent to physicians with incomplete charts • Electronic signature capability speeds deficiency release • Automatic deficiency release	More complete chart documentation; reduced follow-up requirements on MR staff; more efficient turnaround of patient bills	Turnaround of deficient charts; FTE requirements for medical records staff; # of days required for billing; # of days to reimbursement
Large FTE commitment required for medical records processing, coordination with other departments	• Automatic assignment of unique medical record number; built-in controls prevent duplicated numbers • On-line access to MPI from all points of admission/registration • System shares data with ADT, case mix, and patient accounting modules	Accurate database for medical records, admissions and registration, patient accounting staff reduces amount of necessary information seeking, frees staff time for other activities	FTEs required for information-gathering activities
Manual chart and deficiency tracking resource intensive, error-prone	• Chart deficiency analyses by physician, category, or age of deficiency • Automated chart-tracking capabilities	Frees FTE time; improves access to medical records information; facility more aware of deficiency types and sources	FTE time commitment; amount of time to locate chart; turnaround of deficient charts

(Continued on next page)

Patient Financial and Administrative Systems (Continued)

Problem to Be Addressed	Technology Feature/Functionality	Projected Benefits	Benefit Measurement Criteria
Medical Records (Continued)			
Medical records coding does not capture full range of diagnoses or procedures for patients; hospital revenue does not reflect actual provision of service/ patient population	• Maintenance of appropriate, on-line DRG groupers • Coding indexes and edits for procedures, physicians, diagnoses, morphology codes, pathology records; irregular discharges and complications • Ability to handle multiple diagnoses, procedures, or physician codes per patient	Coding capabilities optimize reimbursement per patient; accurate coding helps ensure timely payment by payers	$ revenue per patient/member
Scheduling			
Facility has difficulty responding to unexpected scheduling dilemmas (i.e., down equipment, ill staff)	• Electronic review of schedules, by resource type and location • Automated system allows remote appointment scheduling	Minimized delays from unexpected events preserve pretest regimens; reduce patient wait time; improve patient satisfaction; opti-mize use of facility resources	Time required to reschedule patients; # of patients able to reschedule
Inefficient use of facility resources; complex interactions between ancillary departments affect productivity, volume	• Provides multiple-level, multiple-request scheduling by facility, clinic, service, physician, technician, equipment, and room • Accommodates user-defined scheduling parameters (i.e., appointment types, duration, and available time slots) • Provides availability of productivity, utilization, and statistical reporting • Allows decentralized (i.e., by department) as well as centralized scheduling	More efficient use of resources reduces number of canceled appointments; wait lists optimize patient volume; facility able to support more complex testing interactions, supporting continuum of care activities	# of canceled appointments; total volume of appointments by department
Lack of information in ancillary departments delays scheduled appointments, testing	• System produces medical records "pull" slips, double appointment notifications, encounter forms, copy forms (if applicable), and appointment registration reports • On-line views available by physician, clinical, resource • On-line look-up of specific patient • System generates appointment schedule list by provider, patient, or time schedule	Improves communication between ancillary departments and clinics	# of appointments delayed due to missing information, paperwork

Patient Financial and Administrative Systems (Continued)

Problem to Be Addressed	Technology Feature/Functionality	Projected Benefits	Benefit Measurement Criteria
Scheduling (Continued)			
Scheduling conflicts delay provision of care	• System alerts to potential appointment conflicts (patient as well as health care resource) • On-line scheduling capability includes schedule modifications or updates, on-line search for appointment time availability within designated parameters such as day of week, hour of day, duration, room • On-line review of available provider time slots to schedule patients	More efficient delivery of services speeds care, improves patient and provider satisfaction	Patient LOS; # of conflicts resulting in delay of care
Utilization Review/Quality Assurance (UR/QA)			
Staff time commitment in tracking/evaluating UR/QA cases	• Electronic compilation of survey records • Ad hoc report writer capabilities allow hospital-defined management and statistical reporting • Free text capability for on-line entry of UR/QA data • Generates printed assignments for QA review	Reduced/eliminated redundant paperwork frees staff to concentrate on other care activities; electronic compilation of data facilitates reporting, reduces time necessary to produce required reports	FTEs required to track UR/QA, produce reports
UR/QA functions not meeting facility's needs for timely identification of potential patient care problems/overstays; requires heavy staff time commitment to track and identify UR/QA cases	• Maintenance of ICD-9 and other specified diagnosis-approved LOS data • Automatic assignment of estimated patient LOS at admission • Concurrent review of hospital-defined QA parameters • On-line display of LOS data with indicator denoting need for review • Accommodates user-defined criteria for UR/QA patient reviews	Increased efficiency in identifying and tracking UR/QA cases; more timely identification of potential overstays and patient care problems; improved quality of care; better performance on regulatory reviews	FTE required to identify/track UR/QA; # of identified UR/QA cases

Decision Support Systems

Problem to Be Addressed	Technology Feature/Functionality	Projected Benefits	Benefit Measurement Criteria
Clinical			
Inconsistent patient care across or within physician patient populations	Clinical decision support allows on-line maintenance and support of enterprise-accepted protocols of care, including: • Variance reporting • Diagnostic and treatment prompts	Standard treatment of like patient groups facilitates consistent, high-quality care; variance reporting facilitates enterprise UR/QA	% variance from protocols; patient outcomes
Inconsistent treatment patterns	Clinical decision support provides on-line diagnosis and treatment support through prompts and alerts to variance from protocols	More consistent treatment; increased physician education and awareness	% variance from protocols; patient outcomes
QA program unable to monitor entire volume of patient events and care	Rules-based processing alerts to patient events: • That should always occur in combination • That should not occur in combination • That should occur in sequence	Automated support assists in maintaining quality and preventing care errors	# of cases identified as possible QA problems; # of cases affirmed as QA problems
Research support for care protocol development is not systematically available, information manually compiled and evaluated	• Clinical decision support system allows relevant data (patient and cost) capture • Automated data analysis capabilities; protocol can be edited or changed on an as-needed basis	Ongoing data collection and protocol evaluation allows fluid, best-case practices to constantly be incorporated into established protocols, keeping care standardized and costs low and clearly identified	Revenue per member per month; cost variations within DRGs; inpatient cost per day; patient outcomes
Financial/Administrative			
Facility executives have little time to make complex and far-reaching strategic decisions	• System modeling functions perform sensitivity analyses, goal seeking, and multiple variable forecasting • Capability to perform complex "what-if" analyses • System allows executives to personalize start-up, display information • Provides risk analysis capabilities, based on entire patient populations or entire episodes of illness • Information organized by strategic business unit or cost center • Combines flexible procedure costing, sponsor composition, and contract payment rates and case-mix reporting functions in one integrated database	More rapid data access, in combination with more advanced data analysis techniques, provides reliable support for decision makers in determining strategy and setting organizational policies	Financial strength, quality of care

Decision Support Systems (Continued)

Problem to Be Addressed	Technology Feature/Functionality	Projected Benefits	Benefit Measurement Criteria
Financial/Administrative (Continued)			
Facility unable to identify exact costs of patient service lines, facilities	• System supports multiple types of accounting • System supports case-level and product line costing	Improved identification of costs supports both strategic and operational decisions about services, facilities	Clearly identified costs by facility, service line
Lack of advanced financial data support and analysis hinders facility capability to make financial and strategic decisions in a timely fashion	• System allocates actual expenses to procedures, based on usage parameters • System maintains multiple cost categories for allocations and analyses • Supports multiple allocation techniques (e.g., simultaneous equations, single and double stepdown) • Maintains standard costs and volumes for statistical and comparative reporting purposes • On-line and departmental product and service line budget assumption definitions • Interface with general ledger for current and pro forma reporting • Allows definition of relationships between capital/operational budgets, between product line and departmental statistics for forecasting purposes • Incorporates historical data	Cost accounting capabilities provide accurate costing information for analysis; supports costing studies, contract compliance audits, and retroactive simulations associated with potential managed service contracts; flexible budgeting capabilities enhance ability of facility to focus on product line and variable budgeting; improve department/product line managers' understanding and profit/loss responsibility; decrease time requirements in preparing complex budgets	Financial strength
Separation of cost and clinical data requires manual compilation of information for case-mix analysis	• System supports multiple patient care planning categories (PPCs) • Users can access PPC data and appropriately edit • System provides support for multiple groupers • System provides consistent, reliable reports analyzing volumes by financial class, geographic origin, DRG, physician, and program specialty • System monitors profitability and utilization on case-by-case and summary basis	Automated case-mix analysis supports rapid and effective decision making, based on timely and accurate historic facility data; system provides common database for planning and statistical analysis	Financial strength

(Continued on next page)

Decision Support Systems (Continued)

Problem to Be Addressed	Technology Feature/Functionality	Projected Benefits	Benefit Measurement Criteria
Financial/Administrative (Continued)			
Time commitments necessary to access and compile necessary reports manually	Ad hoc reporting capabilities allow multiple, flexible reports and formats, including: • Medicare to total population • FTE, division comparisons • Admissions by service area • Physician performance • Inpatient versus outpatient populations • Revenue versus expenses	Timely access to critical business and medical information, fewer FTEs required for compilation	FTE savings
Time-consuming effort to reassign patient groups to physicians	System can identify patient group, match to available/qualified physicians	Efficient resource reapportionment should physician suddenly become unavailable; improved levels of service to patients	Speed of access to data; physicians/patients matched by qualifications, specialties, availability

Provider Managed Care Systems

Problem to Be Addressed	Technology Feature/Functionality	Projected Benefits	Benefit Measurement Criteria
Authorization/Eligibility			
Delays in authorization and eligibility verification through manual efforts; or high number of rejected payments because of ineligible or unauthorized procedures	• On-line eligibility and authorization capabilities (EDI) • System supports membership contract terms, dates, and PCP information • Tracks authorization requirements and status	Speeds initiation of patient care, with associated positive impact on patient-satisfaction levels; reduces staff requirements (time and FTEs) for verification (i.e., letters, phone calls) activities; reduces paper use; increases cash flow	Amount of time required to verify patient authorization/eligibility; # of FTEs dedicated to authorization/eligibility; paper volumes and costs; # of claims rejected because of ineligibility/lack of authorization
Claims, Reporting			
Delayed reimbursement of managed care accounts	Automated generation of patient bills, considering: • Diagnosis and services • Contract terms, including loss limits • Payer billing requirements, standard forms On-line tracking of payment status per contract, per patient EDI links with payers allow electronic claims submission, reimbursement	More accurate and timely managed care billing; adherence to managed care contract terms, including loss limits, electronic claims submission, and reimbursement speeds, and stabilizes cash flow, minimizes staff resource requirements; automated tracking of accounts needing follow-up speeds payment and reduces required FTE efforts	Average managed care account A/R days; revenue from managed care contracts; FTE requirements for contract management
High % of claims rejected or returned on initial submission	• System automatically formats claims in payer-preferred format • "Holds" incomplete claims for review and completion	Increased % of claims paid on initial submission; reduced required follow-up; stable or more predictable cash flow from submitted claims	% of claims paid upon first submission; FTE time spent in follow-up; postage, phone costs
Time commitment for preparing manual reports for Medicare, Medicaid, managed care payers	• On-line maintenance of information, ad hoc reporting • EDI capabilities allow electronic submission of reports	Reduced time requirements for report preparation; reduction in forms printing and storage costs	Time in FTE required for reports preparation; cost of forms printing and storage
Contract Management			
Inability to audit managed care contract compliance; costs of rebilling underpaid charges	• System automatically verifies patient eligibility under terms of contract • System tracks patients exceeding "stop-loss" terms in contract • Provides claims tracking, monitors payer compliance with terms; rebilling and appeals processes • On-line verification of payment status	Adherence to terms of managed care contracts optimizes revenue; more efficient tracking of information identifies revenue-producing and revenue-losing contracts; automated audit capabilities allow organization to accept more managed care business without losing revenue	$ per member per month; ratio of FTE/managed care contracts; contract profitability

(Continued on next page)

Provider Managed Care Systems (Continued)

Problem to Be Addressed	Technology Feature/Functionality	Projected Benefits	Benefit Measurement Criteria
Contract Management (Continued)			
Inability or difficulty in identifying advantageous potential managed care contracts	• Users can perform what-if analysis to determine financial ramifications of incorporating service rate charges, adding stop losses and high-cost pass-through items • Tracks contract revenue, cost and utilization by payer group, physician, diagnosis, and patient • System provides modeling for contract plan changes, profitability, and negotiations	Increased ability to target and negotiate most advantageous contracts and terms	$ revenue per member per month
Lost revenue from inability to audit terms of managed care contracts	• System automatically rolls up actual billings versus managed care contract terms • System automatically calculates patient copays against terms of managed care contracts	Adherence to terms of managed care contracts optimizes revenue; accurate cost information allows more effective contract negotiation with less FTE time for preparation	# of FTEs dedicated to contract management and negotiation; revenue from managed care accounts

Payer Managed Care Systems

Problem to Be Addressed	Technology Feature/Functionality	Projected Benefits	Benefit Measurement Criteria
Authorization/Eligibility			
Authorization/referral process is difficult for contracted providers to understand and navigate; health plan staff unable to quickly provide answers to contracted providers	• System provides referral control mechanisms for primary care physicians, specialists, and hospital-based providers • System automatically compares authorization requests against contract terms	Routine authorizations and referrals are quickly processed; improved ability of health plan FTE staff to respond to requests; increased provider and patient satisfaction with health plan	Time to complete routine authorization/referral requests
Tracking and communicating current eligibility to contracted providers is time-consuming	• System automatically generates eligibility lists at user-defined intervals • System supports provider capability to verify eligibility electronically	Reduced FTE commitment to routine eligibility issues; increased provider satisfaction through ease of electronic verification processes	FTEs for eligibility verification; volume of electronic verifications; contracted provider satisfaction
Billing and Medical Economics			
Large FTE resources required to generate and monitor premium billing activities	• Group and individual premiums are calculated automatically according to contract terms • Contract riders are tracked and communicated automatically	Higher productivity of FTE staff charged with premium billing activities; consistently accurate and timely billing according to contract terms	FTEs for premium billing/# of contracts to be billed; # of billing errors
Difficult to effectively set contract rates for differing populations	• System collects, allows manipulation of actuarial rate-setting data • Reporting capabilities allow utilization reporting and analysis of profit/loss by group	Improved ability to determine fiscally appropriate premiums; reduced avoidable contract loss	Profit/loss by contract
Claims			
Claims adjudication policies inconsistently applied across contracts, locations	System automatically adjudicates claims, according to health plan–defined policies and procedures	Adjudication policies are evenly applied to all contracts and members; reduced legal exposure for health plan	Of adjudicated claims, # resolved outside of contract/adjudication guidelines
Evaluating and paying claims requires large FTE commitment; manual process slow and error-prone	• System automatically evaluates and pays claims, with and without risk withholds • Ability to accept claims electronically, in plan-preferred formats	Claims FTEs more productive, allowing more focus on difficult or unusual cases; increased ability to support managed care contracts adding minimal FTEs	Claims FTEs/claims volume; minutes per claim for evaluation and payment

(Continued on next page)

Payer Managed Care System (Continued)

Problem to Be Addressed	Technology Feature/Functionality	Projected Benefits	Benefit Measurement Criteria
Contract Management and Support			
Difficult to administer capitated contracts with multiple providers and provider groups	• System automatically generates member rosters for each contract • System automatically calculates risk pool withholdings • System calculates year-end risk pool settlements based on user-defined contract terms	More accurate capitated contract administration; fewer FTE resources required to administer capitated contracts; increased communication and accuracy with contracted providers leads to possible corresponding increase in provider satisfaction	FTEs required for capitated contract administration activities; $ from capitated contracts; # of capitated contracts being supported
Difficult to effectively track and compare expected versus actual contract utilization	• System stores patient demographic and historical data; contract terms/fee schedules/authorizations • Reporting capabilities allow flexible data comparisons: case mix by provider/contract; initial and final diagnoses; procedures performed	Improved ability to compare expected versus actual utilization; improved knowledge positions health plan to more appropriately set rates and evaluate contracts	Profit/loss by contract; expected/actual utilization by contract

Clinical Systems

Problem to Be Addressed	Technology Feature/Functionality	Projected Benefits	Benefit Measurement Criteria
Documentation, Nursing			
High levels of nursing overtime to complete routine documentation	Point-of-service technology allows real-time charting	Increases care documentation; nurses walk fewer miles (patient room to terminals); increase in patient satisfaction, as staff spend more time physically with the patient	Completeness of documentation; OT hours logged by nursing staff; # of miles walked by nurses
Inconsistent or incomplete documentation of assessments, progress notes, patient histories	• On-line charting of assessments, progress notes, patient history • Point-of-care technology available directly from patient location	Improved documentation; information is consistently collected and legible to other caregivers; redundant entry is eliminated; fewer delays in care due to unavailable or illegible information; reduction in errors due to unavailable/illegible patient information; reduced need for forms	FTE time savings (entry, follow-up); # of repeated care activities (i.e., assessments, tests); # of avoidable errors; patient LOS; form costs (printing & storage); dictation/transcription costs; # of delays in surgical/testing procedures due to inaccessible information; FTE $ for delayed procedures
Nursing recruitment, retention difficulties	• Nursing system reduces required OT to complete necessary care documentation • Care path prompts conform with nursing "best practices"	Freed clerical time allows more direct care activities, less demands on personal lives; on-line prompts and alerts facilitate nurse education, confidence	Average length of nursing service; # of unfilled, but recruited, nursing positions
Nurse time spent on routine, repetitive care activities and charting	Automated interfaces capture patient vitals (i.e., temperature, blood pressure, pulse) and enter into patient record	Nursing staff spend more time on nonroutine care activities; increase in job satisfaction; recruiting and retention	Time on direct care activities; average length of nursing service; # of unfilled, recruited-for positions
Poor documentation leading to errors, poor or failed regulatory reviews	• On-line charting capabilities • Care planning/pathway variance alerts • Automated data capture of routine patient data • Automatic dosage calculation capabilities	Increased accuracy and timeliness of patient care documentation; improved performance on regulatory reviews (i.e., JCAHO, NCQA)	Documented errors due to illegible or inaccessible information; scores and results of regulatory examinations
Medications			
Difficult to access data through course of routine patient care	• System located at patient bedside • System interface provides access to orders, results, progress, and chart notes	Bedside access to patient information reduces unnecessary repeat testing; facilitates timely provider diagnosis and treatment decision making	# repeated tests due to unavailable data; patient LOS; delays in care due to inaccessible data

(Continued on next page)

Clinical Systems (Continued)

Problem to Be Addressed	Technology Feature/Functionality	Projected Benefits	Benefit Measurement Criteria
Medications (Continued)			
Inappropriately high drug costs	With MD order entry: • System provides alternative (suggestions) to prescribed medications • Prompts for most effective durations of administration and dosages • Interface with patient administrative data verifies patient-specific reimbursement guidelines	Increased physician awareness of drug costs, best-practice course of treatment; lower patient costs	% of accepted generic alternatives; $ savings on pharmaceuticals
Lost patient charges	System provides automated bedside charge capture	Recouped revenue previously lost through administrative error	$ revenue from patient charges
Medication errors, through incorrectly calculated doses	Point-of-care system automatically calculates correct dosage	Reduces medication errors	# of medication errors
Nosocomial infection rates	Order-entry system prompts for best-practice course of treatment	Reduced nosocomial infection rates	# of nosocomial infections; % variance from best practices
Orders, Results			
Duplication of tests due to inaccessible test results	On-line results reporting; staff can remotely access system for results from tests and procedures	Cost savings from fewer repeated tests; courier savings from fewer trips with results; lower LOS for patients	# of duplicated tests; # of courier trips; patient LOS
Frequently lost orders, unnecessary test repetition	On-line inquiry for outstanding orders	Fewer lost orders, shorter patient LOS	# of procedures repeated due to administrative delay; patient LOS
Frequent scheduling conflicts, test delays	• Order explosion notifies ancillary departments upon order • System flags duplicate orders	Better scheduling/ optimized use of ancillary department resources	# of procedures repeated due to administrative delay; volume of tests performed; length of time between order and test; # of avoidable scheduling conflicts
Incomplete or inaccurate orders	• On-line order verification • On-line order change capability • On-line inquiry for completed, pending, deleted, or canceled orders • Ability to place orders on hold pending RN, MD, pharmacist approval • Standard order set capability	Complete and accurate orders	# of complete, accurate orders

Clinical Systems (Continued)

Problem to Be Addressed	Technology Feature/Functionality	Projected Benefits	Benefit Measurement Criteria
Orders, Results (Continued)			
Lack of coordination between orders, lab, pharmacy, patient data	System checks order, lab, pharmacy, patient data, alerts to conflicts	Improved interdepartmental communication; reduced ADEs	# of ADEs; # of medically unnecessary tests
Lost test charges	• On-line verification of order, charge • On-line charge capture	More complete and efficient capture of patient A/R data; clear identification of facility costs	Increased revenue from tests
Order requisition forms expensive, difficult to track	Automated order entry	Reduced/eliminated requisition forms	$ savings, form purchases
Test results and interpretations dictated and transcribed, with copies to chart, physician, testing department (i.e., lab, radiology)	• Results and interpretations entered directly to on-line patient record • Access to record from all appropriate providers and departments	Reduced FTE requirements for dictation and transcription; reduced forms requirements due to on-line access capabilities; information accessible at all times to appropriate providers; improved documentation of care	FTE costs, dictation and transcription; forms costs (printing and storage); # of delays in care because of inaccessible information; patient LOS; # of repeated tests
Time spent verifying orders	Direct physician order entry with electronic signature capability/auto-authentication	Time savings for staff following up to verify written, faxed orders	# of orders requiring verification
Pathways, Protocols			
Clinical pathways and protocols are inconsistently adhered to by facility staff	• On-line pathways and protocols • Interactive variance alerts when protocol/pathway is deviated from • Reporting capabilities allow analyses of variance by type, location, staff	Variance alerts stimulate immediate problem response by caregiver; reporting capabilities allow further research and evaluation of pathway/protocol	# of caregivers using pathways protocols; reports of variance and explanation
Critical pathways in development at scattered sites; protocols, care, and treatment plans are manual	On-line critical pathways, including care plans and access to care protocols	Facilitates case management across continuum of care; standardized treatment for similar patients increases quality of care, reduces cost; identified "average" treatment costs provides more accurate data for managed care contract negotiation	Revenue per member per month; cost variations within DRGs; managed care contract rates versus actual costs; inpatient cost per day; patient outcomes

(Continued on next page)

Clinical Systems (Continued)

Problem to Be Addressed	Technology Feature/Functionality	Projected Benefits	Benefit Measurement Criteria
Pathways, Protocols (Continued)			
Inconsistent nursing evaluation and management of patient care	Care pathways and automated care planning incorporate enterprise treatment standards treatments; prompt nurse actions and reactions	Increases nursing ability to evaluate and manage patient care; standardizes treatment; improves quality of patient care	Patient outcomes; variance from established treatment plans/protocols

Home Health Systems

Problem to Be Addressed	Technology Feature/Functionality	Projected Benefits	Benefit Measurement Criteria
Accounts Receivable/Billing			
Time-consuming for staff to collect data and generate UB-92, HCFA 485-7 forms	System pulls relevant data from patient files; automatically generates UB-92, HCFA 485-7	Increased productivity in generating required reimbursement forms; potential positive impact on cash flow	FTE time required to generate UB, HCFA forms; volume of forms produced before system compared with after implementation
Clinical Documentation, Care Planning			
Incomplete, late, or otherwise inadequate documentation affecting claims approval, payment	• System allows input of automated visit notes at the time of visit • System holds standard assessments (ADL, SF-36) • System care plans document procedures that should be performed; allows comparisons with procedures actually performed	Improved clinical documentation; possible reductions in rejected claims, with corresponding improvement in cash flow	# of claims rejected for inadequate documentation
Inconsistent treatment patterns are affecting care quality, financial impact of cases with similar requirements	System allows for standard care plans by type of illness, with exception reporting and substantiating documentation	Improved clinical documentation; more consistent treatment patterns; increased predictability in financial and clinical resources required	Variance against established care plans
Managed Care			
Delayed reimbursement of managed care accounts	Automated generation of patient bills, considering: • Diagnosis and services • Contract terms, including loss limits • Payer billing requirements, standard forms On-line tracking of payment status per contract, per patient EDI links with payers allow electronic claims submission, reimbursement	More accurate and timely managed care billing; adherence to managed care contract terms, including loss limits; electronic claims submission and reimbursement speeds and stabilizes cash flow, minimizes staff resource requirements; automated tracking of accounts needing follow-up speeds payment, reduces required FTE efforts	Average managed care account A/R days; revenue from managed care contracts; FTE requirements for contract management
High % of claims rejected or returned on initial submission	• System automatically formats claims in payer-preferred format • "Holds" incomplete claims for review and completion	Increased % of claims paid on initial submission; reduced required follow-up; stable or more predictable cash flow from submitted claims	% of claims paid upon first submission; FTE time spent in follow-up; postage, phone costs

(Continued on next page)

Home Health Systems (Continued)

Problem to Be Addressed	Technology Feature/Functionality	Projected Benefits	Benefit Measurement Criteria
Managed Care (Continued)			
Time commitment for preparing manual reports for Medicare, Medicaid, managed care payers	• On-line maintenance of information, ad hoc reporting • EDI capabilities allow electronic submission of reports	Reduced time requirements for report preparation; reduction in forms printing and storage costs	Time in FTE required for reports preparation; cost of forms printing and storage
Scheduling			
Scheduling conflicts delay provision of care	• System alerts to potential appointment conflicts (patient as well as health care resource) • On-line scheduling capability includes schedule modifications or updates, on-line search for appointment time availability within designated parameters such as day of week, hour of day, duration, room • On-line review of available provider time slots to schedule patients	More efficient delivery of services speeds care, improves patient and provider satisfaction	# of conflicts resulting in delay of care

Ancillary Department Systems

Problem to Be Addressed	Technology Feature/Functionality	Projected Benefits	Benefit Measurement Criteria
Laboratory			
Delays in laboratory procedures affecting timely delivery of patient care	• Audit trail of each collection list or collection label set requested • Generates a "specimen-obtained" list for nursing units once draw times and dates are entered • Tracks specimen collection status (facility-defined) • Free text entry for documenting reasons a specimen was not collected • Generates specimen redraw lists • On-line inquiry for patient test orders and results	Better specimen control decreases number of lost specimens; minimizes delay when redraw is necessary	Patient LOS; # of lost/uncollected specimens
Detailed administrative and procedure data tracking requires large FTE commitment	• Generation of user-defined collection lists, labels, and work sheets at user-defined intervals • Automatic assignment of accession numbers to specimens upon generation of the collection list or receipt of the specimen in the lab • Centralized accessioning of specimens to facilitate result inquiry and sharing of specimens across multiple lab sections • Generation of facility-defined system control reports (e.g., outstanding specimens, cumulative outstanding results, master patient log) • Capability for workload statistics reporting • Surgical pathology results reporting, automatic SNOMED coding, patient history files	Increased productivity; optimized use of facility and staff resources	Volume of procedures to staff ratio
Difficulty in capturing laboratory-related patient charges	• Electronic capture of patient charges; interface with patient accounting feeds data automatically • Ability to batch-update the charge master file (i.e., standard % increase to all procedure codes)	Increased, more accurate charge capture	# of identified charge errors; $ revenue from laboratory procedures
"Normal" and "abnormal" laboratory values and ranges inconsistent across enterprise	• Enterprisewide laboratory information system allows standardized, condition-specific diagnosis of values and ranges • On-line alerts when values fall outside defined parameters	Improved quality of care through alert system, standardized treatment of like patients; reduced costs of care; better identification of costs supports financial, managed care organizational functions; fewer unnecessary test repeats	Patient outcomes; patient LOS; # of unnecessary test procedures

(Continued on next page)

Ancillary Department Systems (Continued)

Problem to Be Addressed	Technology Feature/Functionality	Projected Benefits	Benefit Measurement Criteria
Laboratory (Continued)			
Time-consuming compliance with FDA regulatory reporting	• System automatically tracks required substances and devices • Reporting capabilities in FDA-preferred formats • Supplier provides regular updates, as regulations are modified/introduced	Less required FTE time to comply with regulatory reporting requirements; more complete, accurate reporting	Timely submission of required reports
Pharmacy			
Difficulty in tracking patient charges for medications	Interface with patient administrative system captures patient charges	More timely and accurate billing for pharmaceuticals; fewer lost patient charges	$ revenue
High pharmacy inventory costs	Automatically updates inventory with on-line adjustments and transfers for floor and pharmacy stock	Reduced necessary inventory; less clerical time required to track medications	Space required for inventory; on-hand inventory value; clerical pharmacy FTEs
High or increasing number of medication errors; easily avoidable adverse drug reactions, interactions	• System provides access to pharmaceutical reference systems and patient medical record data • System provides on-line alerts to drug interactions, contraindications • Screening of drug interactions, allergies, IV incompatibilities, and duplicate orders • On-line calculation of IV therapy drip rate	Proactive quality of medication orders, reducing potential adverse drug reactions or interactions, medication errors	# of adverse drug reactions, interactions, medication errors
Long lead time to fill or delays in filling prescriptions or prescription refills	• Interfaces between systems allow access to both medication and progress note information • On-line alerts for incomplete information, potential quality problems • Order-entry system feeds prescriptions electronically	Improved patient satisfaction through time savings; pharmacy staff has head start on necessary follow-up; improved accuracy (fewer errors) of completed orders through alerts, access to complete patient and pharmacological information	Patient wait time from arrival at pharmacy to in-hand order; # of delays due to illegible or incomplete prescriptions
Resource intensive to track/rotate expired inventory	• System tracks location and status of inventory	Less FTE time required for inventory management; fewer wasted $ on expirations	FTE time spent on inventory control; $ value of expired inventory
Time-consuming compliance with FDA regulatory reporting	• System automatically tracks required substances and devices • Reporting capabilities in FDA-preferred formats • Supplier provides regular updates, as regulations are modified/introduced	Less required FTE time to comply with regulatory reporting requirements; more complete, accurate reporting	Timely submission of required reports

Ancillary Department Systems (Continued)

Problem to Be Addressed	Technology Feature/Functionality	Projected Benefits	Benefit Measurement Criteria
Pharmacy (Continued)			
Time spent in preparing materials and drugs given in combination	System allows materials and drugs typically given in combination to be stocked together	Reduced time required between prescription of drug treatment and administration of medication(s)	Time spent searching out necessary materials
Radiology			
Difficulty in tracking patient charges for radiology services	• Automatic generation of charges for equipment • Charging can automatically be activated at time of order entry or results reporting • Electronic billing capability • Interface with patient administrative system captures patient charges • Generate physician charges to support physician billing	Better financial/service tracking decreases number of lost charges, increases revenue	$ revenue for radiology services
Historical views inaccessible to caregivers	• Capability to retain and report current location of each study for multiple film storage areas or for film checkout • Assigns unique radiology number for first patient visit • On-line maintenance of file film data	Historical information supports improved decision making, quality of care; better patient outcomes	Patient outcomes
Lost or duplicate radiology records causes patient delays, administrative complications	• Assigns unique radiology number for first patient visit • On-line maintenance of file film data • Generates film removal slips for insertion on patient film jacket • Generation of radiology flash cards and film jacket labels on request • Capability to retain and report current location of each study for multiple film storage areas or for film checkout	Better radiology file film identification, tracking; ease of review from remote locations	# of lost/duplicate radiology records
Surgery			
Frequent staff or resource conflicts in OR scheduling result in patient delays, underutilization of surgical staff or facilities	• System provides estimated procedure time • On-line scheduling capabilities allow changes and cancellations	Improved scheduling efficiency reduces labor costs (clerical FTEs as well as surgical staff scheduled, but not used); increased effective use of OR	Clerical FTEs required for scheduling; staff FTEs left idle because of scheduling conflicts/ delays; surgical volume

(Continued on next page)

Ancillary Department Systems (Continued)

Problem to Be Addressed	Technology Feature/Functionality	Projected Benefits	Benefit Measurement Criteria
Surgery (Continued)			
	• Automatic alerts to potential conflicts in schedule date, time block, suite, surgeon, anesthesiologist and equipment assignment • Automatic display of information necessary to complete scheduling process (i.e., surgeon preference, lists, special conditions/requirements for the surgical procedure) • Audit trail tracks changes, cancellations, and additions • Provides printed OR schedules	resources (staff, equipment, locations) optimizes patient volume, revenue; efficient scheduling improves patient satisfaction	
High or increasing time and labor costs in coordinating surgical materials, tracking patient charges	• System maintains surgeon preference lists, with materials and amounts required for each scheduled procedure • Organizes item information including cost, location, usage, vendor, and ordering quantities	Improved tracking of revenues and costs, patient charges; time savings in coordinating required materials for surgical procedures	$ revenue from surgical procedures; FTE time required for materials/supply coordination
OR time and resources not being used to maximum cost efficiency	• Allows for supply/resource costing by DRG • Availability of productivity, utilization, and statistical reporting	Increased active control and monitoring of utilization capabilities and patterns	Cost benefit comparison of DRG cost to generated revenue; surgical procedures and revenue
Significant amounts of FTE time spent on prepping surgical suites; or frequent late starts because of unprepared suites	• System maintains surgeon preference lists, with materials and amounts required for each scheduled procedure • On-demand reporting lists scheduled procedures	Increased effectiveness in preparing surgical suites for procedures	Prep time required per procedure type; # of late starts due to unprepared OR

Sample Emerging Technology Oversight Group Charter

Chapter 3 discusses the study and adoption of emerging health care information technologies. To gain the most benefit from these technologies (while aggressively managing the risks), many organizations charge a specific group of individuals with program and project oversight and direction.

This appendix presents a sample charter for such a group, called here the Emerging Technology Oversight Group (ETOG). The charter covers the group's purpose, responsibilities, reporting and meeting requirements, and typical membership. The purpose of the charter is to codify why the group exists, what it has been charged with accomplishing, and who is to be included in the emerging technology oversight process.

Emerging Technology Oversight Group Charter

I. Purpose

There are numerous potential organizationwide and departmental uses of technology that must be considered in the course of information technology planning efforts. As such, the primary objective of the Emerging Technology Oversight Group (ETOG) is to coordinate the strategic and tactical use of emerging technology at <<facility>> in support of organizational goals and objectives.

The ETOG receives its authority to operate from the Information Systems Steering Committee, and will act as a standing recommendation body. The ETOG will supervise the activities of the Technology User Group (TUG), and will delegate responsibility as appropriate.

II. Responsibilities

The Emerging Technology Oversight Group (ETOG) was created to define <<facility>> requirements for the use of unproven technologies, and identify acceptable risk/return ratios for financial investment. In addition, the

ETOG is charged with monitoring the ongoing scope and success of emerging technology investments, investigating as appropriate the feasibility of broadening the use of successful technologies.

Specific objectives of the ETOG include:

- Establish a vision for the use of emerging technologies at <<facility>>
- Provide specific recommended direction regarding the potential financial, clinical, and administrative application systems that are relevant to the use of emerging technologies at <<facility>> and its affiliated entities
- Approve draft feasibility plans and provide recommendations regarding adoption, including establishing priorities and specific project activities
- Review and approve an economic (cost/benefit) methodology by which emerging technology investments will be judged
- Review and provide recommendation for the use of capital to be invested in emerging technologies; evaluate project capital requirements in terms of overall <<facility>> capital requirements and availability
- Review information assembled regarding specific emerging technology functionality, risks, and benefits
- Establish and review the activities of the Technology User Group (TUG) charged with carrying out individual project-by-project feasibility and research activities
- Guide education and awareness efforts for emerging technologies at <<facility>>
- Coordinate the use of emerging technologies with the vision and goals set forth in the organizational information systems long-range plan
- Review information assembled by the TUG regarding specific application system functionality and benefits

III. Membership

The following positions and departments shall be represented in the membership of the ETOG:

- Chief information officer (cochair)
- Chief financial officer (cochair)
- Information systems department
- Medical records
- Service line representatives, including (as appropriate):
  - Ambulatory services
  - Surgical services
  - Intermediate and long-term care services (i.e., home health, SNF)
  - Inpatient services
    Ancillary clinical services (i.e., laboratory, radiology, pharmacy)
  - Health plan services

- —IPA/MSO representatives
- —Academic department representatives
- Patient administration
- Clinical staff (physician, RN, others)
- Case management
- Risk and utilization review

IV. Reporting Structure

The ETOG shall report to the Information Systems Steering Committee and the chief executive officer on an as-needed basis. ETOG-developed materials will be utilized in this reporting process.

V. Meetings

Meetings shall be held monthly. Meetings shall be conducted by the chairperson, and a standard agenda (as designed by the ETOG) shall be followed.

VI. Administrative

Minutes shall be taken at each meeting. Minutes shall be distributed to each member of the committee, and to administration for review and comment. At the start of each meeting, the prior month's minutes shall be reviewed and approved, or changes may be recommended for approval by the committee.

VII. Attendance

Attendance by all committee members is strongly encouraged. Your participation and input are vital to the continued success of <<facility's>> emerging technology investments.

Glossary

Alpha development site: The first place where new software is tested in a true operational environment. Not all technology vendors use this term; some refer to all test hospitals as *beta sites*.

American National Standards Institute (ANSI): A national organization that acts as a clearinghouse for voluntary standards in a variety of industries, including health care.

Ancillary department systems: These technologies manage activities internal to individual hospital departments, such as laboratory, radiology, pharmacy, and the operating room.

Application software: A computer program that carries out a specific business or personal task, such as registering a patient, processing an order, or producing a bill.

Architecture: The general technical layout of a computer system.

Artificial intelligence (AI): A knowledge-based computer capability in which the computer either actually mimics the thought process of a human being or in some way generates new knowledge. See also *expert systems*.

Best practices: An IT management method, also called *benchmarking,* in which the plans and activities of outside organizations successfully using a technology are studied for possible adoption or modification. Also sometimes referred to as *systems use audits*.

Beta site: Refers to the client facility where new software is tested once alpha-site testing has been completed. Beta testing focuses on the ability of the vendor to install and support software without the assistance of the software designers. Some vendors do not differentiate clearly between alpha- and beta-site testing.

Breakthrough benefits: Fundamental investment returns gained through engineering new and more efficient methods of executing work and patient care processes.

Bundled: A method of pricing in which the supplier charges one price for hardware, software, and implementation services, leaving the buyer with fewer choices of components and levels of service than if the supplier's wares were unbundled.

Business value: The benefits an investment (in information technology) is capable of returning. Contrasts with *specific utility.*

Capitated reimbursement: A reimbursement mechanism that guarantees providers a fixed payment for each "covered life" per month. The fixed fee is paid regardless of the intensity and level of services provided.

Central processing unit (CPU): That part of a computer that includes the circuits controlling the interpretation and execution of instructions.

Central service organization: An organization that assumes responsibility for a particular set of functions for associated IDS provider organizations. These may include information systems, managed care contracting, centralized business or financial processing, and/or materials management.

Chief information officer (CIO): Organizational executive charged with strategic and operational direction of information systems. Not all facilities include this position; however, the responsibilities related to IT must still be performed.

Client/server: A computer data and software interaction configuration that takes advantage of distributed processing power to improve computing speed and end-user capacity.

Clinical data repository (CDR): A database that holds patient demographic, financial, and clinical information on-line, with enterprisewide (IDS) data access and input.

Clinical systems: These systems contribute to the direct management of patient care activities, including order entry, results reporting, acuity classification, and case management.

Clinical workstation: The final component of the electronic medical record, clinical workstations are typically client/server based, intended to support data management activities by those providing patient care.

Community health information network (CHIN): An arrangement among numerous entities (provider, payer, regulatory agency) to share and exchange common data.

Computer: A digital or electronic device that carries out logical activities, computations, data manipulation, and text editing under the direction of a set of instructions called a *program*. Major components of a computer include its control circuitry, main memory, and CPU.

Computer system: A computer plus peripherals, software, and procedures.

Conversion: The process of shifting from one system to a different system, even if both are supplied by the same vendor.

Core competency: A fundamental skill. In the JDA practice, this term is used to refer to particular skills that are basic and expected throughout the organization. As IT consultants, we consider projects related to the basic information systems life cycle as our core competencies—long-range planning, vendor selection, and systems implementation. Contrasts with *distinctive competency.*

CPU: See *central processing unit.*

Critical cluster architecture: An architecture allowing a logical grouping of database and end-user requirements to form a solution for a business or medical service function or set of functions. By definition, a cluster must be supported by a single supplier, operating on a uniform hardware platform. Contrasts with *single-supplier architecture.*

Custom development: The development of application software by provider organizations to meet specific needs and requests. This approach provides greater flexibility and control at a greater financial and risk burden. It is supported by advanced technical tool sets, including object-oriented programming systems. This continues to be necessary for certain levels of intrasystem data exchange, although the use of *interface engines* is reducing this need.

Database: (1) Any collection of data. (2) Data stored in a computer in a particular organizational structure and for a particular purpose.

Database machine: A computer whose sole task is to maintain a database and control access to it.

Database manager: (1) Data-processing professional specifically trained to control the operation of a system's database. (2) A piece of software that coordinates internal database activity. Also called *database management system,* or *DBMS.*

Decision support systems: These technologies allow providers to collect and analyze data in more sophisticated and complex ways. Activities supported include case mix, budgeting, cost accounting, clinical protocols and pathways, outcomes, and actuarial analysis.

Distinctive competency: A defining skill set not widely held by peer group members. This positions the organization to offer aggressive, proactive value to customers. Contrasts with *core competency.*

Dumb terminal: A monitor with no processing capability of its own that simply sends input to a computer and displays the information the computer sends back.

Electronic data interchange (EDI): The automated exchange of data and documents in a standardized format. In health care, some common uses of this technology include claims submission and payment, eligibility, and referral authorization.

Electronic mail (e-mail): A means of sending letters, memos, and other correspondence electronically through a network.

Electronic medical record (EMR): This technology, fully developed, meets provider needs for real-time data access and evaluation in medical care. Together with *clinical workstation* and *CDR* technologies, the EMR provides the mechanism for longitudinal data storage and access.

Emerging technology: Technology unproven or untested in the health care industry, offering great potential benefits to investors willing to accept associated risks.

Expert systems: These systems provide the ability to consolidate a predefined set of rules (from one or more experts) into an application system. These rules are then used to process a unique data set against predetermined variables. Used in medical diagnosis, clinical information, credit, and risk assessment systems.

Facilities management: An approach to IT management through which a provider organization enters into a contract with a third party for management or operational IT support. In contrast to *outsourcing,* provider organizations choosing this approach typically maintain their own data center and capital equipment; the facility management firm manages the people and processes relating to IT.

Fulcrum™ Series methodology: A specific approach, developed by JDA, to managing and optimizing the use of information systems technology.

General financial systems: These technologies work to support the basic financial transactions required in the day-to-day operation of a health care enterprise (for example, general ledger, payroll, materials management, human resources).

Hardware: Equipment that runs application software, or peripheral devices (for example, printers, computer monitors) used in working with computers.

Health level 7 (HL7): A data interchange protocol for health care applications that simplifies the ability of different vendor-supplied systems to interconnect. Although not a software program in itself, HL7 requires each software vendor to program HL7 interfaces.

Health maintenance organization (HMO): An organization that acts as both payer and provider of health care services for a defined patient population.

Home health systems: Application software designed to support the administrative, financial, and clinical activities relating to home health care.

Hospital information system: An integrated system that automates the administrative, financial, and clinical aspects of patient care.

Incremental benefits: Benefits that add simple or moderate value to current work and patient care processes.

Information systems (IS): Application software designed to automate a particular subpart of the health care process, such as managed care administration, laboratory operations, or patient administration.

Information technology (IT): Technology designed to facilitate process automation in health care. A broader term than *information systems,* IT encompasses application software, operating systems, database/data access systems, telecommunications (networks, telephones) equipment, and computer hardware.

Integrated circuit: A piece of semiconductive material that contains interconnected, miniaturized electronic circuits. Also called a *microchip.*

Integrated delivery system (IDS): A health care provider organization offering support for the majority of care across the continuum, incorporating physician groups and focusing on the management of patient populations.

Also called *integrated health delivery network, integrated health network,* or *regional delivery system.*

Integrated systems: An information systems architecture in which all system components share a common logical or physical database.

Interface: Specialized software and/or hardware that permits the passing of information back and forth between two systems. Interfaces may be either batch or on-line.

Interface engines: Application systems and hardware that facilitate data transfer and communication between disparate systems.

Internet: A worldwide network of computers that developed out of a U.S. Department of Defense program. Today, it is privately administered and maintained, and is used for multiple purposes, including communications, education, and commerce.

Investment return cycle: The period between investing in an information technology and realizing positive benefit returns. The *incremental benefits* cycle may be as little as one-half the time as the *breakthrough benefits* cycle.

IT-driven reengineering: Effort through which procedures and work flow are redesigned to interact more effectively with existing and planned IS technologies. Through this process, organizations can potentially extend the life and effectiveness of IT investments.

Knowledge-based system: See *artificial intelligence* and *expert systems.*

Local area network (LAN): A communications network linking all system devices within a specific area, such as a department or building floor. A defining characteristic of a LAN, compared to alternative methods of interconnecting a network, is flexibility in adding devices or changing the systems configuration. With a LAN, such activities involve plugging and unplugging devices from preplanned wall jacks and entering instructions into the LAN's file server. With other approaches, adding devices or reconfiguring involves pulling cable.

Long-range plan (LRP): Articulated 3- to 5- year strategies and tactical plans to address the technological implications of an organization's business and medical service objectives.

Main memory: Memory built into the computer itself. Programs and data reside in the main memory for short periods just before going into, or just after coming out of, the CPU. The more main memory a computer has, the more "powerful" it is; that is, the more computations it can do in a given period. Also called *random access memory,* or *RAM.*

Mainframe: A very large computer.

Maintenance/service agreement: A contract detailing the responsibilities of the vendor or a third party for repairing hardware or correcting software problems.

Managed care systems: Technologies providing support for the multiple and complex contracting arrangements required under managed care reimbursement. Some managed care systems are designed to support health care provider activities relating to managed care; others work with activities of health care payers.

Memory: Any device for storing information in a way that allows direct access to the information by a computer. Usually, the term refers to either the storage circuitry built into the computer for short-term storage (main memory) or a system's disk drive or drives.

Minicomputer: An intermediate-size computer with less storage, power, and speed than a mainframe. A minicomputer can run the same kinds of applications as a mainframe.

Networking and telecommunications: These types of technologies allow humans and machines to communicate across geographic distances. Specific technologies include local and wide area networks, telephone systems, EDI, and data interface applications.

Office automation: Utilization of computers and computer networks to accomplish tasks associated with white-collar activities, such as word processing, spreadsheets, e-mail, and message processing.

Open-systems architecture: An approach to IT development that allows interoperability betweeen hardware and software components regardless of the orginating developer/supplier.

Operating system: Software that controls the internal operations of a computer, such as the allocation of main memory, as opposed to software, which actually performs tasks.

Operations unit: The group within the IS department responsible for supporting the classic data-processing functions of an organization. In most organizations, this unit keeps systems operating 24 hours per day, 7 days per week.

Optical fiber: A thin strand of glass wire capable of carrying encoded beams of light. Besides this "optical" method of transmission, two other major ways of conducting signals from one point to another are through wires or cables via electronic signals, and through the air via electromagnetic radiation (for example, radio waves, infrared radiation).

Optical storage: Storage (and retrieval) of data on a disk coated with light-sensitive material. Reading and writing information are done via a laser. Optical storage is at least two orders of magnitude more efficient than magnetic-disk storage. It is not the same as video storage.

Outsourcing: An approach to IT management through which a provider organization enters into a contract with a third party for management or operational IT support. The provider organization does not maintain control of IT assets and typically does not maintain a data-processing center. See *facilities management.*

Packaged software: Technology that is fully developed and tested in operational environments, and is available for commercial purpose.

Parallel processing: (1) A computer design technique in which a problem is broken into many pieces and worked on simultaneously by more than one processing unit working in tandem. (2) During a systems conversion, running both the old and new system at the same time until it is established that the new system is working to specifications.

Patient financial and administrative systems: These technologies deal with the practical, nonclinical aspects of treating patients (for example, admissions, registration, scheduling, quality assurance/utilization review).

Patient interactive systems: These technologies allow patients to interact directly with a provider's information system, regardless of the patient's physical location. These applications support administrative functions such as appointment scheduling and account balance inquiries, as well as clinical functions such as answering questions and receiving care instructions.

PBX: See *private branch exchange.*

Personal computer (PC): A relatively inexpensive computer that users can operate after a few hours of training.

Point-in-time analysis: Evaluation of and reaction to an immediate need or situation; sometimes occurs because of management failure to proactively forecast and plan for likely future needs or requirements.

Practice management systems: Application software designed to support the financial, administrative, and clinical activities relating to physician group practice.

Private branch exchange (PBX): Originally used to refer to a device for switching the voice signals of a telephone system, the term now is often used to mean a device capable of switching voice and data signals. Also called *digital PBX* and *digital switch.*

Proprietary: Limited to utilization by a single vendor. A proprietary chip is an electronic circuit a hardware maker designed for its own use instead of utilizing off-the-shelf technology.

Qualitative benefits: Benefits logically inferred to have resulted from use of a technology, but difficult or impossible to tie directly to the technology.

Quantitative benefits: Financial benefits clearly measurable and attributable to the use of a particular technology.

Random access memory (RAM): See *main memory.*

Regional delivery system: See *integrated delivery system.*

Remote processing: A network configuration in which a data center is removed from the main user areas, as in another building or geographic location.

Report writer: A computer language specifically designed for accessing a database and generating custom reports.

Request for information (RFI): A short, high-level document used to collect basic system data as well as vendor marketing literature in some vendor selection projects.

Request for proposal (RFP): A document commonly utilized by provider organizations during vendor selection projects. Some organizations feel the RFP, typically binary and extremely detailed, can be a long and cumbersome instrument through which to select a vendor.

Response time: (1) Time lapse between data entry into a computer system and acknowledgment of data receipt. (2) Time lapse between a vendor maintenance call and initiation of actions to solve the problem.

Return on investment (ROI): The quantitative and qualitative benefits realized by an organization from an investment in information technology. Benefits may or may not be economic in nature; they also may be strategic in nature, positioning an organization for future benefits.

RFI: See *request for information.*

RFP: See *request for proposal.*

Risk disposition: The level of risk an organization's management is willing to support in making IT investments. Determined by both the structural characteristics of the provider organization and the management team's orientation toward risk and reward.

Security: Tools and techniques used to protect a computer system from unauthorized access.

Shared system: A computer configuration in which more than one organization uses the same programs running on the same hardware, all of which are maintained at a central data center. Not to be confused with *remote processing.*

Single-supplier architecture: The purchase of most or all applications from a single health care–specific software supplier. Contrasts with *critical cluster architecture.*

Software: Computer programs to control internal computer operations or to carry out the tasks for which an information system is designed. See also *application software* and *systems software.*

Source code: Software that is developed in machine language. Also called *object code.*

Specific utility: How well the capabilities of an investment (in information technology) are being used by an organization. Contrasts with *business value.*

Strategic benefits: Positioning or other benefits that may offer substantial value to the organization, but will not necessarily have a direct impact for some time to come.

Supercomputer: A very fast computer (faster than a mainframe), intended primarily for supporting scientific research and handling massive amounts of data.

Superminicomputer: A minicomputer with capabilities approaching those of much larger computers.

Systems integration: Technical and functional programming activities that develop connectivity between legacy systems and new technologies.

Systems life cycle: The process through which an investment is planned, selected or developed, implemented, utilized, then reevaluated. Activities within the life cycle are geared to optimize and retain the highest rate of return for the investment for the longest period of time.

Systems software: A computer program that enables the computer to control its own internal operations, such as controlling the coming and going of data, allocating space in main memory, or logging user activities. Also called *systems program.*

Systems unit: This unit, operating with the IS department, works to develop, implement, and (sometimes) customize application software in use by the provider organization.

Systems use audits: Activity in which the *best practices* use of technology is compared to an organization's use, with the goal of increasing the use and value of current information systems.

Technical support unit: This unit, operating within the IS department, is typically responsible for general PC support and hardware or cabling plans and changes.

Telecommunications: See *networking and telecommunications.*

Telemedicine: The use of telecommunications technology for medical purposes, including clinical consultation, education and training, and administrative teleconferencing.

Transparent interface: Systems interfaced in such a way that to the user they seem integrated. Also called *seamless interface.*

Turnkey: One way that software vendors package their product in which all software, hardware, and installation costs are included in a single price.

Theoretically, the vendor does all the work, and the customer just "turns the key" to start successful system operation.

Unbundled: The discrete pricing by a supplier for hardware, software, and implementation services, enabling a buyer to "pick and choose" which components and levels of support it wants to purchase. The opposite is *bundled.*

Unix: A type of nonproprietary operating system that can operate several different brands of computers without modification.

Vendor selection: Activities through which an organization purchases an information systems technology. The vendor selection process quantifies desired organization benefits and objectives, and defines technical and operational system requirements.

Vendor system proposal (VSP): A document, issued to potential vendors, that gathers functional, cost, and strategic information about a firm and its products. The VSP is not as detailed as an *RFP,* but is more detailed than an *RFI.*

Version: The current edition of a piece of software. Sometimes called *release.*

VSP: See *vendor system proposal.*

Wide area network (WAN): A communications network linking computers, system devices, and LANs that are dispersed over a large geographical area, such as in a medical center or university campus.

Workstation: An intelligent terminal or PC designed for specific users in a specific industry. A workstation includes special software and certain peripherals.

Index